THE GRENADA DOCUMENTS

With an Introduction by

SIR ALFRED SHERMAN

Explanatory Notes by

BRIAN CROZIER

THE SHERWOOD PRESS

First published 1987

Introduction © Sir Alfred Sherman 1987
Explanatory Notes © Brian Crozier 1987

The Sherwood Press Ltd, 88 Tylney Road, London E7 0LY

ISBN 0 907671 27 6

Printed in Great Britain by Redwood Burn, Trowbridge, Wiltshire

CONTENTS

EDITORIAL NOTE

Although a selection of the captured Grenada documents released by the US Department of State and Department of Defense was distributed in London and other European capitals through the United States Information Service in September 1984, this book is the first analytical and annotated compilation to be published in Britain.

Since the appearance of the American official 'overview and selection' a number of books based wholly or in part on the Grenada documents have been published in the United States. The most useful of these, from the standpoint of the student of communist affairs, is *The Grenada Papers*, edited by Paul Seabury and Walter A. McDougall, with a Foreword by Sidney Hook (Institute for Contemporary Studies, San Francisco, 1984). This excellent compilation was, however, naturally aimed at an American readership. The present book was prepared with British and other West European readers in mind.

The text of the selected documents has been left unchanged and uncorrected. In cases where typing or other errors obscured the meaning, we have tried wherever possible to provide clarification in the accompanying notes.

Other American books consulted include: *The Revolution Lobby*, by Allan C. Brownfeld and J. Michael Waller (Council for American Security and Inter-American Security Institute, Washington, DC, 1985); *American Intervention in Grenada*, edited by Peter M. Dunn and Bruce W. Watson (Westview Press, Boulder, Colorado, 1985); and *Revolution and Intervention in Grenada*, by Kai P. Schoenhals and Richard A. Melanson (Westview, 1985).

CHRONOLOGY

13 March 1979
Grenada United Labour Party (GULP) government of Sir Eric Gairy overthrown in nearly bloodless coup inspired by Maurice Bishop's New Jewel Movement (NJM). Formation of 'People's Revolutionary Government' (PRG).

30–31 August 1979
Grenada admitted to membership of the non-aligned movement.

October 1979
Twenty people arrested in alleged plot to overthrow PRG. Conservative newspaper *The Torchlight* ordered to suspend publication on charges of publishing material likely to cause civil unrest. New press law bans owners of *The Torchlight* from recommencing newspaper publishing operations.

3 November 1979
More than thirty people arrested on discovery of second alleged coup plot in three weeks. 'Great amounts' of arms and ammunition seized. Supporters of Sir Eric Gairy accused.

December 1979
Eight former members of Gairy government's 'mongoose gang' ('police aides') convicted on charges of attempted murder. Sentences range from 12 to 16 years. Release of 20 detainees.

1 April 1980
Further 15 detainees released.

1 May 1980
Three persons arrested and 15 members of People's Revolutionary Army (PRA) suspended in alleged plot to seize a military camp and stage a coup. Those involved said to be 'ultra-leftist' elements aiming to establish what PRG described as 'an unworkable socialist State'. Alleged links with marijuana cultivation and North American crime syndicates.

May 1980
Under a treaty signed in Moscow by deputy Prime Minister Bernard Coard, Soviet long-range reconnaissance aircraft allowed to land at new airport at Point Salines.

June 1980
Maurice Bishop, other members of PRG, Governor-General Sir Paul Scoon, and Cuban Ambassador to Grenada narrowly escape assassination when time bomb explodes. Bishop describes bombing as 'a monstrous crime committed by imperialism'. New recruitment drive for People's Militia announced.

2 October 1980
Prevention of Terrorism Law promulgated, with death penalty for acts of political violence resulting in death.

17 November 1980
Five shot dead in Northern Grenada during attack on militia camp at Sauteurs. Sporadic guerrilla activities.

1 January 1981
Speaking at a conference of Commonwealth foreign ministers, Bishop accuses the US of trying to overthrow his government, citing a three-stage plot by CIA.

19 June 1981
Closure of mimeographed independent newspaper, *The Grenadian Voice*.

20 June 1981
Newspaper (publications) Law promulgated banning the launching of any new newspaper in Grenada for one year pending formulation of a

'media policy' to meet the needs of a 'revolutionary society'. This left the State-owned weekly *The Free West Indian* with virtual monopoly.

11 July 1981
Four members of 'Gang of 26' arrested in connection with a 'CIA plot to overthrow the government'.

August 1981
Formation of a Patriotic Alliance of Grenadian exiles opposed to PRG, but unconnected with Eric Gairy. On 20 August Bishop sends message to UN Secretary-General Kurt Waldheim and certain heads of foreign governments charging Reagan Administration with intention to invade Grenada. Allegations denied in Washington. On 26 August Bishop described recent UN and NATO exercises in Caribbean as a 'practice run' for an invasion of Grenada.

January 1982
Twenty-four detainees, including former deputy Prime Minister in Gairy government, Herbert Preudhomme, released. Richard Luce, UK Minister of State for Foreign and Commonwealth Affairs, on visit to Caribbean, expresses British government's 'concern' over 'considerable number of political prisoners in Grenada', and its hope that PRG will 'vigorously pursue' its stated objective of holding elections and introducing a new Constitution.

6 February 1982
Speaking at a meeting in Barbados with five East Caribbean leaders, President Reagan accuses Grenada of having joined with Soviet Union, Nicaragua and Cuba in promoting Marxism in region.

April 1982
Grenada alone among members of the Caribbean Community, (CARICOM), supports Argentina in conflict with Britain over the Falkland Islands.

26–8 July 1982
Bishop signs wideranging economic and political agreements in Moscow.

October 1982
Bernard Coard resigns from NJM Central Committee at a plenary meeting at which Bishop is attacked.

16–18 November 1982
Third meeting of CARICOM in Ocho Rios, Jamaica. Grenada's PRG criticised for failing to hold elections or bring detainees to trial.

14 October 1983
Maurice Bishop ousted and placed under arrest in a coup led by Bernard Coard and 'General of the Army' Hudson Austin.

17 October 1983
Austin announces expulsion of Bishop from NJM Central Committee for having 'disgraced the party and the revolution'. Several ministers arrested.

19 October 1983
Crowd of 3000 marches on barracks to free jailed ministers, but driven back. Up to 200 deaths reported. Army declares that Bishop and other ministers died during exchange of fire, but most reports claim they had been executed by firing squad. A 96-hour curfew proclaimed by military authorities.

20 October 1983
Revolutionary Military Council created under chairmanship of General Austin. Killing of Bishop provokes widespread criticism, including protest from Cuba.

21 October 1983
Emergency session of Organisation of East Caribbean States (OECS) to discuss situation in Grenada. Decision to 'take appropriate action'.

23 October 1983
At emergency meeting of Caribbean leaders, Jamaica and Dominica announce breaking of diplomatic relations with Grenada, and Grenada's suspension from membership of CARICOM.

25 October 1983
US operation 'Urgent Fury' begins when 1,500 members of 82nd Airborne division and 400 Marines land on Grenada, with stated intention of taking control of communications networks and guaranteeing safety of several hundred US medical students. Substantial resistance from 1,500-strong People's Revolutionary Army and some Cuban construction workers. In letter to Congress, President Reagan says decision to intervene was taken in response to a request from the OECS. British Prime Minister Mrs Margaret Thatcher tells House of Commons that government had 'communicated to the United States their very considerable doubts . . . about initiating action . . .'

26 October 1983
Miss Eugenia Charles, Prime Minister of Dominica and Chairman of the OECS, tells UN Security Council that Sir Paul Scoon had asked for help on 21 October.

27 October 1983
Fighting ends in St Georgia's, the capital. Sridath Ramphal, Commonwealth Secretary-General, calls for withdrawal of US forces and replacement by peacekeeping force from Commonwealth member countries.

30–31 October 1983
Austin and Coard taken prisoner by US forces and held on board the ship *Guam* before being transferred to prison on Grenada on 6 November. Official US casualty figures announced: 18 dead, 86 wounded and one missing. All 603 US medical students evacuated.

3 November 1983
US Permanent Representative to UN, Mrs Jeane Kirkpatrick, declares that Mrs Thatcher had 'misunderstood the whole basis of our action'.

3 December 1983
General election in Grenada. The New National Party (NNP), recently formed conservative group led by Herbert Blize, wins 14 of the 15 seats. Provisional government, styled 'Advisory Council', established by Governor-General Scoon in aftermath of October 1983 intervention, was thereupon dissolved.

UNLEARNED LESSONS FOR GRENADA: SOVIET IMPERIAL EXPANSION'S NEW PHASE

by Sir Alfred Sherman

Future historians will ascribe greater significance to the Grenadian sequence of 1979–84 than our own governments and current affairs commentators have done. Apart from a brief burst of media coverage during the American landings in Grenada, the island has received little attention. Yet it is rich in lessons, epitomising as it does a new phase in Soviet imperial policy.

Western media and chancelleries were reluctant to face up to Grenadian developments and their wider significance before the death of the Prime Minister, Maurice Bishop, and the American intervention which it precipitated. After a period of embarrassed recognition of the post-landing situation, much of it compulsively critical of the United States, the world's governments and media have reverted to their former reticence, reflecting an attitude shared by American media and Congress with other Western observers by which news which cannot be made to rebound to the Reagan Administration's discredit is no news at all.

This tells us as much about the state of mind in Western countries as it does about Grenada. But as part of a pattern of response towards expansion of the Soviet sphere of influence in Europe, Asia, Africa and the Caribbean Basin during the second half of this century, its intrinsic relevance makes it as much a part of the Grenada story as what happened on the island itself, 'the Grenada for us', of which 'Grenada in itself' is only one ingredient.

The pattern is composed of life-cycles. First, each new revolutionary movement is greeted with enthusiasm by Western 'liberals'; its glowing promises are contrasted with shop-soiled reality. The never-never land syndrome of our political Peter Pans is triggered off. They compulsively reject demonstration of the new regime's communist origins

1

or connections as 'McCarthyite smears', 'anti-communism' or similar epithets, implying meanness of spirit. After the full nature of communist control and Soviet involvement has become apparent, differentiation occurs inside the 'liberal' mass. One tendency suffers temporary disillusion before surrendering to the irresistible call of the next Shangri-la, as the compulsive gambler does to his next dead cert: this time will be different.

The second tendency blames the West for having driven the reformers into the arms of the Soviets, irrespective of the facts of the case, using such catch-all slogans as 'self-fulfilling prophecy'. A third cites the transformation and Soviet political success as a further argument for seeking a 'political solution' to Soviet–Western differences. Yet a fourth argues that if it is lavishly aided, the new regime might yet be detached from the Soviet orbit and become a 'new Tito', ignoring the consideration that Moscow drew far more lessons from the Tito episode than our own masters have done.

Grenada reproduced this pattern quite faithfully until the crisis of 1983. The coup, counter-coups, riots and killing of Bishop spurred an otherwise passive United States Administration into action. Had Bishop been demoted or killed quietly, and had the United States not happened to have embarked a force of marines destined for the Lebanon, where it lacked any clearly defined politico-military objective and could therefore easily be spared for Grenada, it seems most likely that Grenada's final slide into satellitedom would have been achieved smoothly. By now it would have completed its assimilation of arms and training and be in a position to threaten other islands of the Eastern Caribbean, and to serve as a base for guerrilla operations against Venezuela when the time became ripe again.

There was no inevitability about the United States landings, no advance planning, very little intelligence work. Much of the information contained in the documents published here could have been obtained and in some cases made public during the four years of Bishop's rule. The United States Administration has yet to adduce systematically the lessons of Grenada and other cases of advanced long-distance Sovietisation. The British Foreign and Commonwealth Office has still further to go than that; it has yet to recognise that the American landings were at all justified, let alone for the best.

The first stage of Soviet imperial expansion, extending Soviet borders and creating satellites, including North Korea, and occupying eastern Austria and northern Iran, had remained close to what Lenin had laid down for Poland and Central Asia. Socialism was to be imposed by the Red Army; local communists were only auxiliaries, and dispensable at that; the communised countries' rulers kept on as short a leash as the Soviet rulers judged politic taking all factors into account. (The world balance of power subsequently led to the unconditional withdrawal of Soviet troops from northern Iran, and with it the collapse of the Soviet-imposed regime, and to the conditional withdrawal of Soviet forces from Austria, in return for Austrian neutrality.)

The lesson of Iran, and of the failure of communist insurrection in countries such as Malaya, Burma and Indonesia, brought about a second phase in Soviet imperial strategy. It took greater account of obstacles in the path of intellectual, political and insurrectionary communisation, and sought instead to build working alliances with new States and with anti-colonial movements. Policies towards countries as different as Egypt, Syria and Iraq, Ghana and Guinea, and Burma, showed a mixed pattern. Great-power clientisation was given precedence over efforts to bring social and political structures closer to the Soviet model. Their communisation was sacrificed to military and diplomatic considerations, even if this entailed throwing local communists to the wolves.

The third stage, a breakthrough towards remote-controlled satellisation, came about more by accident than by design; but the Kremlin showed itself adept at recognising and exploiting opportunities when they occurred.

Cuba is well documented as a revolution which began as 'bourgeois' and was opposed as such in its early days by the official Communist Party, with whom Fidel Castro and his brother Raúl had close relations, but later became communised by a reverse take-over. Satellisation did not follow automatically. For some years, Fidel Castro was an ally of the Soviet Union, not a satellite. He rebuffed Soviet attempts at interference, bringing about the recall of a Soviet ambassador in 1962 and purging his party of veteran communist cadres who tried to take the first steps towards curbing and eventually ousting him. Against Soviet advice and wishes, he initiated armed uprisings in Venezuela, Bolivia and Uruguay among others. These were at first resisted by the established communist parties there, which felt obliged to join later, when the excitement of armed action was enticing away many of their supporters, only to regret this later when the uprisings collapsed.

Satellisation came later, thanks partly to Cuba's economic dependence on the Soviet Union and partly to the moulding of a whole generation of cadres in the armed forces, secret police and party by Soviet training.

Though the 'liberal' press hailed Castro's revolutionary achievements in economics and welfare, in fact hairbrained economic policies led to an early decline in living standards, welfare and education. This generated dependence on Soviet aid, without which Castro would have faced levels of discontent difficult to suppress on an island lying just off the United States and Central America.

It is a sobering thought that the Soviet Union can afford economic aid on this scale only thanks to Western loans and other economic assistance to the Soviet bloc given with government encouragement partly in the belief that it would reduce Soviet aggressiveness, whereas it predictably increased capacity for expansion while leaving appetites unchanged. Substantial British and West European loans to Cuba, which are most unlikely ever to be repaid, have also made it easier for Castro to maintain the loyalty of his military and civilian cadres. This is particularly relevant in the light of the part played by economic discontent in bringing about the internal conflict, which led to Bishop's murder, which in turn precipitated the American landing.

Whereas the communisation and subsequent satellisation of Cuba was played out in front of the television cameras, a parallel process in South Yemen has received little attention. The British government chose to hand over the Aden Protectorate to a Marxist-infiltrated anti-Western terrorist movement, when it could equally well have handed over to its supporters among the Sheikhs. After satellisation was completed, the Russians instituted purges, killing off the authors of the revolution and replacing them by their own protégés, in order to ensure absolute dependence.

This pattern, to be repeated in Afghanistan and Grenada, harks back to Stalin's purges in the Soviet Union and later the satellites, designed to produce a breed of absolute conformists. Moscow's ability to reproduce this pattern in countries where Soviet armed might could not be imposed directly indicates how far Soviet political techniques have improved since Stalin 'lifted his little finger' and Tito did not fall.

With help from Castro, Moscow repeated long-distance satellisation in Nicaragua, Angola and Mozambique with a fair measure of success, and in Grenada, where original successes were thrown away when subsequent events goaded the United States into military action.

Like Cuba's, the Nicaraguan revolution began as a genuinely popular movement against a discredited government, though the degree of covert communist control was much greater from the outset. By contrast, attempts at overtly communist revolutions, whether with Soviet blessing, as in El Salvador and Guatemala, or without, as in the South American mainland, failed.

What happened in Grenada could happen in many countries the world over. The British had irresponsibly handed over power to an unbalanced petty tyrant, paving the way for revolution. The New Jewel Movement (NJM) was Marxist *ab initio*, and the chain of events initiated by the revolution was wholly predictable, except for the final ineptitude which precipitated American action. But policy-makers in Washington and London were reluctant to recognise the facts and draw conclusions.

Political and strategic arguments used by the United States Administration to justify its action after the event were equally valid for the whole period since 1979, yet the matter received little attention. No contingency plans were drawn up, no current intelligence framework was established. It took the conjunction of Bishop's murder, the reversal of Lebanon policy while the marines were at easy sailing distance from Grenada and Reagan's mood of frustration over setbacks in both Lebanon and Central America, to make the United States turn and bring to bear its unquestioned strategic superiority. It was a close-run thing.

Because Grenada is small and easily encompassable, the events took place within a short time-span, and virtually the whole documentation is at our disposal. The Grenada documents present a neat, rounded and transparent picture of a process which elsewhere must be disentangled and inferred.

The first lesson is that the Russians have assimilated their experience in Cuba, Central America and Southern Africa, and systematised their *modus operandi* for conformity and satellisation. Training for military personnel, party cadres, intelligence and secret police is provided.

In an older imperial tradition, proxies are used wherever possible, reducing the visibility of Soviet personnel and their contacts with the outside word. International specialisation appears to be based on the principle of 'from each according to his ability'. The Soviets provide arms, training inside the Soviet Union and overall control. The (East) Germans reminiscently provide secret police and internal security advice and training. Under the agreement with the North Korean

Government signed in April 1983 the North Koreans were to train special forces, whose potential for brutality is already well attested in Zimbabwe and Mozambique. North Korea is also regarded as the premier training ground for terrorism and guerrilla warfare. Cuba provided engineering, logistical and staff training, and also Party training, 'mutual study of experience in the different fields of party work'.

The Bulgars undertook to train higher cadres in year-long courses and to supervise their practical work *in situ* after the conclusion of their theoretical training. This may reflect Bulgaria's status as the most complaisant of all the satellites. Czechoslovakia was to provide industrial aid and air transport, as it had done for Cuba. The Soviets were thereby largely spared the moral hazards of foreign travel and possible seduction by this island in the sun.

From a reading of the agreements, notes and descriptions it does not appear that Grenadians were expected to learn even Spanish, let alone German, Russian, Bulgarian or Korean. All courses were in English. Nor are we given the impression that these English-language courses were established specially for the benefit of Grenadians. We might not have learned about them had it not been for our access to the Grenada documents, but, now that we have them, ought we not to be more curious about the courses themselves? How long have they been running, and whom else have they been serving? Which African, Caribbean and Asian governments and revolutionary movements made use of them?

By all accounts, Moscow patently set out to cast this network of international subversion, and of political, military and intelligence training and supervision far wider than Grenada. Meetings in Moscow with the North American and English-speaking Caribbean Department of the Communist Party of the Soviet Union (CPSU) outlined the political tasks assigned to the Grenadian Party. This entailed 'serving as a bridge between the CPSU and the Left Parties in the English-speaking Caribbean . . . giving details of the situation in each of these countries'.

It was this involvement which alarmed other Eastern Caribbean governments. With its new level of armaments, instructors and foreign military cadres communist Grenada was due to become stronger than all its neighbours put together; indeed its military capacity would have exceeded that of the whole of the former British West Indies combined.

In all the neighbouring mini-States there exist nuclei of communists, other left-wingers, poverty, alienation and frustration — where, indeed, are they absent in this imperfect world? None of these states has armed forces but only lightly armed police in small numbers.

It would not, therefore, have been difficult for the Grenadians and their supporters *in situ* to take over the islands one after the other. This would in turn have been welcomed and justified by the pro-Soviet anti-American media and politicians, including the communist professionals and the enthusiastic amateurs such as the *New York Times* and *Washington Post* and their equivalents in Britain and Europe. In this context, it is worth noting the NJM boast that 'our North American networks have once again proved their worth ... excellent media coverage of our visit ...'.

But Grenada did not threaten only the Eastern Caribbean mini-States. It lies athwart one major shipping channel of the Panama Canal, the other passing close to Cuba. It is close enough to the Venezuelan coast to permit night-time landings of people and arms under cover of darkness. This facility had been denied the Miristas (Cuban-oriented revolutionaries) during the guerrilla assault they initiated in 1962. At that time, all supplies had to come from Cuba by sea. This called for fair-sized ships, which the Venezuelan Navy and its well-wishers became adept at tracking and apprehending.

Then, Venezuelan democracy defeated the attack. Now, recrudescence of terrorist and guerrilla activity is anticipated before the decade is out following the collapse of COPEI (the Christian Democratic Party) after an orgy of corruption and incompetence, leading one of the world's naturally richest countries into bankruptcy, and the patent inability of its Democratic Action (Social Democratic) successor to undertake structural reform. A Cuban base of operations in Grenada would have multiplied its effects.

Although a communist party and regime in all things, following communist patterns of government and international relations, the NJM was able to penetrate the Socialist International, where it enjoyed, in its own words, great support from the Nordic Parties—which offset the suspicions of the Latins, particularly of the Italians and Portuguese.

Why Scandinavians, West Germans, Dutch and British should have been so gullible—to give them the benefit of the doubt—would require a separate study. Anti-Americanism, left leanings, inverted race prejudice would presumably all have played their part, together with the compulsive naivety which every 'liberal' carries in his knapsack. At all events, conflict inside the Socialist International over this issue remained unsettled when Bishop was purged and the Americans landed.

On the international front, the Grenadian adventure was going very well. This highlights the question which will have been asked pointedly in Havana and Moscow: if all was going so well for them, what went so wrong as to make them lose the New Jewel in their crown? What worm was gnawing away at the rose?

The documents point to calamitous failure on the economic, social and human fronts. Cuban imperialism soon began to irk. However Africans may react to the Cuban pro-consuls, the Grenadians soon began to resent them and their Grenadian subordinates. As a secret Special Branch report on labour problems experienced in construction of the airport—which, *pace* Plessey and the FCO, the Grenadian NJM and Cubans saw primarily in military terms—discloses: 'Almost all the Grenadian workers see Rullow [the Grenadian in charge under the Cubans] as oppressor and hypocrite . . . he fires workers arbitrarily . . . workers feel their jobs are not secure . . . a worker, Cuffi, was fired . . . the workers found the circumstances unjust and uncalled for . . . Rullow shortly after employed young girl in Cuffi's place, and promptly began sleeping with her . . . The advantage Rullow has over the workers is that he can speak Spanish . . . Rullow seems to be involved in a serious level of favouritism . . .'.

As the documents show, economic discontent was rife, in part due to the exaggerated expectations aroused by the revolution, in part to the fact that socialism is even less efficient than most other economic arrangements. Human problems arose because of the basic discrepancy between the Utopian libertarian promises of the revolution and the increasingly totalitarian nature of the regime created by it.

In most communist regimes the 'animal-farm' progression takes place over a long time-span during which antecedent structures, both formal and informal, are eroded, leaving few, if any, channels through which discontent and disillusion can express themselves. In the case of Grenada it all happened within a span of a few years, before people had become reconciled to the new order, but still hankered after what seemed in retrospect fleshpots, and retained sufficient spontaneity to react outside and inside to the new power structure. In the words of the documents themselves, 'better people' began to leave the party or refused to join in spite of the prospect of privileges held out. These developments, in turn, exacerbated conflict inside the ruling movement.

Communism preaches human solidarity but removes inhibitions against the personalisation of differences of opinion and interest. That is why all communist governments and ruling parties ineluctably engage in internecine violence, reflecting the violence they direct against their subjects. The culmination of the conflict inside the NJM is well known. We have yet to gain access to the self-critical analysis which will doubtless have proceeded in Moscow and Havana, but must conduct our own post-mortem. More generous provision of economic resources could certainly have removed much of the economic discontent. Whether any arrangements could have obviated, or even mitigated, the discontent and disillusion generated by the regime's flawed human face is another question.

Quite apart from their totalitarian character, all communist regimes are despotisms which generate petty despotism. The right to ride roughshod over people in the name of revolution easily generates the habit of riding roughshod for personal reasons. Institutionalised nepotism in favour of the Party gives free rein to group and private nepotism. Sexual harassment, nepotism and financial corruption are notoriously blatant in the Soviet Union, because countervailing forces to human frailty which exist in freer countries have been removed there. Absolute power corrupts in small things as in large.

Reading between the lines, one cannot escape the feeling that Cubans and Russians alike looked down on the Grenadians, regarding them as objects of policy, to be humoured where necessary but not to be taken seriously. Though the Soviets and Cubans displayed a sense of imperial purpose not so different from that of capitalist and pre-capitalist imperialism, this was a sense of purpose owed wholly to the imperial power. From the outset, it lacked the sense of duty to the colonised generated by British and French imperialisms. The British colonial official's solicitude towards his charges, whose side he would usually take against authority, perhaps against white settler and British commercial interests, were absent, just as the French had pride in having no colour bar.

But it is worth considering that had it not been for the impact of oil prices, recession and debt crisis on the Western world its continued economic generosity towards the Soviet bloc might have provided resources sufficient to obviate the economic discontent which played its part in the train of events which led to Grenada's liberation by United States forces and the emergence of democratic institutions under American protection.

The part played by Britain deserves full-scale study. The documents throw little light on this, so most of what I say must partake of the nature of *obiter dictum*. We know that the governments of British Caribbean nations were deeply concerned, but that the Foreign and Commonwealth Office failed to make this concern known. It is also known that the Foreign and Commonwealth Office's attitude to the conflict between Cuba and the United States has been close to neutrality. Cuban involvement in Africa was shrugged off by a senior Foreign Office official a few years ago in the course of a private conversation as 'keeping them out of new adventures in Latin America' precisely when they were already involved in Nicaragua, El Salvador and Grenada.

The absence of resident British heads of mission in San Salvador and Managua on the pretext of economy, when far less crucial capitals are manned by diplomats kicking their heels, indicates British attitudes far more graphically than words. True, British policy towards the Central American conflict has been preferable to that of most European members of NATO, but this owes much to Mrs Thatcher's personal intervention.

Though informed interpretation of the media indicated several days before the landings that military action against Grenada was at least on the cards, the British government does not appear to have been informed until President Reagan's *post-factum* call to Mrs Thatcher at 2 o'clock in the morning, with results we know to our cost. A senior cabinet member later said privately that 'had we been told in advance, we should have said: "They are going to do it anyway, they are our allies, so we must support them." But we knew nothing whatsoever till too late'. This led the Prime Minister and the Foreign Secretary, Sir Geoffrey Howe, into a false position from which they found it correspondingly difficult to extricate themselves after the full facts of the case became known.

Even a year after the event, while claiming credit for helping the new Grenadian government, Foreign Office officials still justify their original criticisms of the landings on the grounds that they violated international law, even though the Governor-General, Sir Paul Scoon, denies this.

There is no single international lawyer's view on the landings. But law must serve justice and the common good, not vice versa. Inasmuch as the United States government had a choice between leaving the people of Grenada under murderous totalitarian rule, a threat to their peaceful neighbours and to peace in the hemisphere, or rescuing them and meeting their neighbours' justified concerns, surely something can be said for the choice they made.

The same can be said, *mutatis mutandis*, for the United States and Eastern Caribbean governments' rights and duties under the UN Charter. That the Foreign and Commonwealth Office could not even see that this side of the argument exists can only strengthen the nagging doubts in our mind.

But not only the Foreign and Commonwealth Office is remiss. The Grenada affair is one in a long line—not excluding Algeria and Suez— which indicates that the North Atlantic Alliance cannot be taken for granted by many of its partners. The question is not whether all European members of NATO concur with all United States policies in the Caribbean basin at any given time. These are, after all, in contention in the United States itself. It is whether we accept that communist advances in Central America and the Caribbean Basin are a threat to North Atlantic Security, hence bad for Britain as well as for the United States. Insofar as this is no longer accepted as axiomatic on both sides of the Atlantic, the partnership rests on insecure foundations which stand in urgent need of strengthening.

We do not know the full circumstances of the Foreign and Commonwealth Office's failure to inform the cabinet. After the débâcle of the Argentinian invasion of the Falklands there was an enquiry of sorts, whatever its merits. The manner in which the British government handled Grenada before and during the landings is equally deserving of study.

Grenada remained nominally part of the Commonwealth throughout the episode. That a communist dictatorship closely controlled by the Soviet Union had been established as part of its expansionary drive to the very doorstep of Britain's main ally might be adduced by some as an additional reason for questioning whether this disparate collection of democracies and dictatorships, Christian, Moslem and atheist states has any real existence, and whether it is not a trammel on Britain's role as a modern democracy and member of the North Atlantic Alliance.

However, those powerful groups who indulge in Commonwealth

fantasies as an opium of the top people took a diametrically opposite stand and used Grenada's formal Commonwealth status as a justification for opposing liberation of the island by the United States and its East Caribbean allies. It is worth noting that those influential ruling groups which made such play of the Commonwealth found no time for the democratically elected governments of the Caribbean who took the lead in pressing for action in Grenada in the interests of their own self-preservation. Exaggerated sensitivity to 'Third World' concerns patently does not extend to those countries which wish to develop in freedom and in alliance with other free countries.

The role of the Commonwealth Secretariat, whose head, Sridath 'Sonny' Ramphal, almost automatically sides with the 'non-aligned', i.e. pro-Soviet, bloc, is easy to trace, though the taboos against criticism of the new Commonwealth, symptoms of what Orwell prophetically warned against as the new masochism, remain powerful. The organisation exists and enjoys its considerable diplomatic power only thanks to the licence and benefits granted it by the British government. If these were removed, it would deflate like a monster balloon. Despite the Governor-General's request for United States military intervention there was no lack of attempts here to involve the monarchy as a propaganda weapon against the American landings. This matter, too, needs study.

The part played by influential groups here in undermining Anglo-American solidarity in reaction to the first small reversal of the tide of Soviet advance since the mid-1950s bears a family resemblance to the vast orchestrated campaign to reach 'new understanding' with the Soviet Union under its new ruler, Gorbachev, suggesting that if only 'misunderstandings' could be cleared away, better relations would automatically follow.

The Grenadian episode indicates that improved understanding of Soviet intentions on our part would lead to greater efforts to thwart Soviet expansion. In the light of the consideration that Soviet–Cuban penetration of the Caribbean will not have been ended by the setback in Grenada, that Guyana and Belize on the mainland as well as many islands will remain at risk for the foreseeable future, the role of the Commonwealth within this wider picture needs clarification. On the one hand, it could be seen as a political framework within which Britain can help to defend the United States and its allies in the Caribbean Basin against Soviet imperial expansion. On the other, it may be used as a pretext and front for virtual neutralism and tolerance of Soviet-originated subversion.

One need only glance at a map to see the vital strategic importance of Central America, Mexico, the Panama Canal, the Gulf of Mexico and the Caribbean Basin for American defence. They are, in Clausewitz's terminology, vital space. Further serious Soviet penetration in the region could bring about a basic change of mood in the United States. Isolationism, 'America Firstism' and 'Western hemispherism' would be likely to converge and bring about a shift of military and political emphasis from Europe to the Western Hemisphere. This in turn could easily strengthen the neutralist and despairing appeasing tendencies on this side of the Atlantic, in turn still further strengthening a 'Western Hemispherism' based upon the despairing belief that the Europeans cannot be trusted as allies and are not worth fighting for.

Lecturing to an 'establishment' international studies Institute in Belgrade in 1984 I was able to bring home to them that further communist successes in Central America would intensify the Soviet threat—which they know to be ever-present—on Yugoslavia's own borders. If only one could be assured of finding equal awareness in London and Paris.

In the Caribbean Basin itself the price of security is eternal vigilance. The people of the British West Indies have been dealt a very poor hand by fate. Dragged by force from their African homelands, subjected to centuries of demoralising slavery, catapulted into independence without the necessary political and economic infra-structure, their economies dependent on the goodwill of their former colonial masters, their staple products subjected to subsidised competition from Europe and the United States, suffering from serious diseconomies of scale, these territories are more vulnerable than most to Soviet–Cuban probing. Their predicament merits sympathy. We do not gloat when a hasty venture into Utopianism sours, but are glad that the people of the island turn out to be mature enough to seize their second chance to make good.

The region needs help, most of which will have to come from the United States, which has most to offer and most to lose. But the other colonial powers in the region—British, French and Dutch—have both residual obligations and present interests as members of the North Atlantic Alliance. We must see to it that duty and interest are not overcast by destructive anti-Americanism, even when American handling of its domestic affairs and foreign relations may fall below the ideal standard, and when armed force is used which some would regard as premature, or unnecessary, even though others might with equal logic regard it as belated. In an imperfect world gun-boat diplomacy may be better than no diplomacy at all.

This is an introduction to the documents: there can be no substitute for digging deeply into them. I hope that in time, companion-volumes will be collated from further gleanings. In one sense, this collection depicts a map of hell but, like Dante's, it also points a way upward to the stars.

Grenada is only the third place from which Soviet power has been prised away during decades of expansion. The others, largely forgotten, were Azerbaidjan and Austria. Instead of averting their faces our mentors and masters should be drawing lessons to apply elsewhere.

THE GRENADA DOCUMENTS
Explanatory Notes

by Brian Crozier

The official documents discovered by the American forces who liberated Grenada in October 1983 were of an importance far transcending the size of the island or the number of its inhabitants. It was a discovery comparable in kind if not in degree, to that of the secret archives of the German Wilhelmstrasse or foreign ministry during the Allied advance into Germany in 1945.

In both cases the point was that these were secret State papers, not intended for publication or perusal by the outside world. The role allotted to Grenada as an outpost and staging-base in the Soviet imperial drive had been inferred by some—very few—observers. What could not be inferred from public speeches or official announcements was the scale of Soviet involvement in Grenada, the thoroughness of the conversion of a Caribbean speck on the map into a totalitarian society and the speed of what I term the 'satellisation' process.

Nor were the Soviets alone involved in this process: so were Cuba and Nicaragua (naturally, in the regional context), East Germany, Czechoslovakia, Bulgaria, Vietnam and North Korea. Moreover, the Grenadian regime played an important and hitherto largely hidden or little-known role in subverting and conditioning the American Congress and media in the interests of Soviet policies in Central America and the Caribbean Basin.

There are interesting similarities between the events that precipitated American intervention in Grenada and the situations that had developed earlier in other Soviet satellites, notably in South Yemen (the People's Democratic Republic of Yemen, or PDRY), Ethiopia and Afghanistan. In each, relatively moderate but pro-Soviet leaders or fac-

15

tions were removed and executed, to be replaced by hard-liners.* It has to be said, however, that the Grenada documents provide no precise evidence of Soviet involvement in the removal of Maurice Bishop (who was suitably pro-Soviet and pro-Cuban) and his replacement by the hard-liner Bernard Coard.

As Sir Alfred Sherman points out, Grenada is only the third place from which Soviet power has been removed during decades of expansion. However, in the other instances he gives—Azerbaidjan and Austria—the Soviets had not established sovereign control over a whole country, nor were they evicted by military force. On Stalin's orders, the Iranian communists (whose party was named Tudeh, or 'Masses') had set up the 'Autonomous Republic of Azerbaidjan' in the reassuring presence of the Red Army. When Iran appealed to the United Nations Security Council, in January 1946, and in the face of strong pressure from President Truman, Stalin suddenly withdrew his forces.

Stalin's successors, Bulganin and Khrushchev, astonished the West in 1955 by letting it be known that they were prepared to withdraw their forces from Austria. The State Treaty of 15 May that year, guaranteeing the sovereignty and neutrality of that country, followed. The Soviet decision to withdraw, however, was not reached under Western pressure. It became clear that the underlying reason was a more important Soviet decision, to set up a military alliance in Eastern Europe to counter NATO. Previously, the Soviets had maintained armed forces in Romania and Hungary under peace treaties which declared that these forces were needed 'for the maintenance of the lines of communication of the Soviet Army with the zone of occupation in Austria'. The Warsaw Pact gave Moscow a permanent excuse to keep those forces in Romania and Hungary, and an occupation zone in Austria became irrelevant.

The point I am making is that Grenada is, so far, the only case of its kind: the removal of a communits government in a *sovereign* State by

---

*In *Ethiopia*, on 3 February 1977, seven members of the ruling military council (the Dergue) were shot, giving absolute power to the hard-liner Mengistu Haile Meriam. In *South Yemen*, President Salem Rubaya Ali was overthrown and executed on 26 June 1978, and replaced by Ali Nasser Mohammed. In *Afghanistan* in December 1979 the KGB masterminded the murder of an insufficiently pliant puppet, Hafizullah Amin, who was replaced by the unconditionally pro-Soviet Babrak Karmal, paving the way for the Soviet invasion of his country 'by invitation'.

military force from an outside power. It was therefore, for the first time, a *strategic* reverse for Soviet expansionism, thus demonstrating that the spread of Soviet-style communism to all countries of the world, envisaged by Lenin (and indeed enshrined in the existing 1977 Soviet Constitution) is not, after all, fatally inevitable. (There is a special piquancy in the fact that Grenada is an English-speaking member of the Commonwealth.)

Until 25 October 1983, the strategic advance of Soviet power had seemed inexorable, despite many *tactical* reverses. The distinction between 'strategic' and 'tactical' in this context needs to be clarified. A Soviet–Cuban victory in, for instance, El Salvador would constitute a further Soviet strategic advance, whereas the defeat of the Cuban-supported insurgents by the US-supported government would merely be a tactical reverse for the Soviet side—that is, the denial of a possible strategic advance, not the abandonment of an already acquired position.

In this distinction lies the real significance of Grenada.

The documents presented in this volume constitute a mere fraction of a vast total. I have selected them for their relevance in clarifying and confirming the foregoing analysis. They should be read in conjunction with the Chronology provided. Wherever possible, I have written specific notes identifying the senders or receivers of letters, or the circumstances of individual documents.

BC

1. PACTS WITH SOVIET-BLOC COUNTRIES

The first and most important of the New Jewel Movement regime's Soviet bloc pacts was with the USSR itself and provided for the delivery, free of charge, of 'special and civil equipment' to a value of 10 million roubles. It was dated 27 July 1980 and was supplemented by a Protocol dated 27 October that year, which provided for further deliveries valued at 5 million roubles. During the first three years of the regime, Grenada also concluded agreements with Bulgaria, Czechoslovakia, East Germany and North Korea; and made an informal arrangement under which Cuba agreed to provide equipment 'to help strengthen the operative capacity of the Security Bodies' of Grenada. In addition, the Bishop government accepted offers of political and/or technical training for NJM party students from the Communist Parties of the Soviet Union, Bulgaria and East Germany.

Agreement with USSR
27 July 1980

Top Secret

AGREEMENT

between the Government of Grenada and the Government of the Union of Soviet Socialist Republics on deliveries from the Union of SSR to Grenada of special and other equipment

The Government of Grenada and the Government of the Union of Soviet Socialist Republics,

18

guided by aspirations for developing and strengthening friendly relations between both countries on the principles of equality, mutual respect of sovereignty and non-interference into internal affairs.

proceeding from the desire to promote strengthening the independence of Grenada

and in connection with the request of the Government of Grenada

have agreed upon the following:

Article 1

The Government of the Union of Soviet Socialist Republics shall ensure in 1982-1985 free of charge the delivery to the Government of Grenada of special and civil equipment in nomenclature and quantity according to Annexes 1 and 2 to the present Agreement to the amount of 10,000,000 Roubles.

Article 2

The delivery of the equipment listed in Annexes 1 and 2 to the present Agreement shall be effected by the Soviet Party by sea, at the port of the Republic of Cuba.

The order of the further delivery of the above equipment from the Republic of Cuba shall be agreed upon between the Grenadian and Cuban Parties.

Article 3

The Government of the Union of SSR at the request of the Government of Grenada shall ensure rendering technical assistance in mastering of the equipment under delivery by receiving in the USSR Grenadian servicemen for training in the operation, use and maintenance of the special equipment as well as by sending Soviet specialists to Grenada for these purposes.

The Grenadian servicemen shall be sent to the USSR for training without their families.

The expenses connected with the Grenadian servicemen's training, upkeep, meals in the Soviet military educational establishments as well as with their travel fare from Grenada to the USSR and back shall be borne by the Soviet Party.

The Government of Grenada shall provide at its own expense the Soviet specialists and interpreters with comfortable furnished living accommodation with all the municipal utilities, medical service and transport facilities for the execution of their duties and shall ensure their having meals at reasonable prices at the places of their residence.

The Soviet specialists and interpreters shall not be imposed by any taxes and duties on entering or leaving Grenada and during their stay there. All other expenses connected with deputation of the Soviet specialists to Grenada shall be borne by the Soviet Party.

Article 4

The Soviet Party in periods to be agreed upon between the Parties shall depute a group of Soviet specialists to Grenada to determine expediency, opportunity and scope of rendering technical assitance in the creation of the stationary shop for repair of the special equipment and transport, commanding staff trainer school, training facilities for Armed Forces as well as the deliveries of missing building materials for construction of the storehouses and road.

The deputation of a group of Soviet specialists shall be effected on the terms and conditions of Article 3 of the present Agreement.

Article 5

The Government of the Union of SSR shall ensure free of charge the transfer to the Government of Grenada of necessary technical descriptions, instructions and manuals in standard composition on operation of the special equipment delivered under the present Agreement.

Article 6

The appropriate Grenadian and Soviet organizations shall conclude contracts in which there shall be stipulated the detailed terms and conditions of deputing Soviet specialists, receiving for training

Grenadian servicemen and other services connected with the implementation of the present Agreement.

Article 7

The Government of Grenada shall not without the consent of the Government of the Union of Soviet Socialist Republics sell or transfer, formally or actually, the special equipment, delivered under the present Agreement, the relevant documentation and information or give permission to use the equipment and documentation by a third party or any physical or legal persons but the officials and specialists of the citizenship of Grenada being in the service with the Government of Grenada.

The Government of the Union of SSR and the Government of Grenada shall take all the necessary measures to ensure keeping in secret the terms and conditions of the deliveries, all the correspondence and information connected with the implementation of the present Agreement.

Article 8

The present Agreement comes into force on the date it is signed on.

Annexes 1 and 2 are an integral part of the present Agreement.

Done in Moscow on July "27", 1982 in two originals, each in the English and Russian languages, both texts being equally valid.

FOR AND ON BEHALF	FOR AND ON BEHALF
OF THE GOVERNMENT OF	OF THE GOVERNMENT OF
GRENADA	THE UNION OF SOVIET
	SOCIALIST REPUBLICS
[signature]	[signature]

**USSR–Grenada Protocol
27 October 1980**

Top secret

PROTOCOL

to the Agreement between the Government of Grenada and the Government of the USSR of October 27, 1980 on deliveries from the USSR to Grenada of special and other equipment

The Government of Grenada and the Government of the Union of Soviet Socialist Republics

have agreed upon the following:

Article 1

The Government of the Union of Soviet Socialist Republics shall ensure free of charge the delivery in 1981–1983 to the Government of Grenada of special and other equipment in nomenclature and quantity according to the Annex to the present Agreement to the amount of 5,000,000 Roubles.

Article 2

In all other respects the Parties will be guided by the provisions of the Agreement between the Government of Grenada and the Government of the USSR of October 27, 1980 on deliveries from the USSR to Grenada of special and other equipment.

Article 3

The present Protocol comes into force on the date of its signing.

The Annex is an integral part of the present Protocol.

Done in Havana on February "9th", 1981 in two originals, each in the English and Russian languages, both texts being equally valid.

FOR AND ON BEHALF	FOR AND ON BEHALF
OF THE GOVERNMENT OF GRENADA	OF THE GOVERNMENT OF THE UNION OF SOVIET SOCIALIST REPUBLICS
[signature]	[signature]

Agreement with Bulgaria
(no date)

AGREEMENT

for cooperation between the Bulgarian Communist Party and the New JEWEL Movement of Grenada for the period 1982–1983

The Bulgarian Communist Party (BCP) and the New JEWEL Movement (NJM) guided by their mutual desire for strengthening and enhancing the links of friendship and cooperation between them, for promoting the friendly relations between the Bulgarian and the Grenada peoples, between the People's Republic of Bulgaria and Grenada, in the interest of the unity and cohesion of all progressive and anti-imperialist forces in the world in the struggle against imperialism, for peace, democracy and social progress, have reached agreement on the following plan for cooperation for the period 1982–1983:

I

The Bulgarian Communist Party shall receive:

A. In 1982:

1. A two-member delegation of the New JEWEL Movement for [*illeg.*] days, to become acquainted with the experience of the [*illeg.*] issues of interest to the Party.

Term: second half of the year

B. In 1983:

1. A two-member delegation of the NJM for seven days, to become acquainted with the experience of the BCP on issues of interest to the Party.

Term: second half of the year

The New JEWEL Movement shall receive:

A. In 1982:

1. A two-member delegation of the BCP for seven days, to become acquainted with the experience of the NJM on issues proposed by the BCP.

Term: second half of the year

B. In 1983:

1. A two-member delegation of the BCP for seven days, to become acquainted with the experience of the NJM on issues presented by the BCP.

Term: second half of the year

II

1. The Bulgarian Communist Party shall grant the New JEWEL Movement yearly, 10 allowances for training cadres in the ten-month specialized courses at the Academy of Social Sciences on Management at the Central Committee of the Bulgarian Communist Party.

2. The Bulgarian Communist Party and the New JEWEL Movement shall exchange delegations which shall participate in the congresses, conferences and other major events organized by them.

3. The Bulgarian Communist Party and the New JEWEL Movement shall assist in the promotion of more intensive cooperation between the public and mass organisations in the People's Republic of Bulgaria and Grenada.

4. The Bulgarian Communist Party and the New JEWEL Movement shall carry out mutual consultations and shall exchange regularly publications, bulletins, films and other materials related to the activities of the two parties.

5. The Bulgarian Communist Party and the New JEWEL Movement may reach agreement on initiatives which have not been included in the present Agreement and which, in their opinion, would help to further strengthen and enhance the relations of friendship between the Bulgarian Communist Party and the New JEWEL Movement, between the People's Republic of Bulgaria and Grenada.

III

The present Agreement is drawn up in two copies, each in Bulgarian and in English, both texts of equal validity.

FOR THE BULGARIAN COM-   FOR THE NEW JEWEL
   MUNIST PARTY: MOVEMENT:

[signature]   [signature]

Note from Czechoslovakian Embassy
(no date)

EMBAJADA DE GRANADA EN CUBA

Sta. AVENIDA No. 8409 Esq. 84   Telefonos:
MIRAMAR, CIUDAD HABANA   29-5429
    CUBA   29-3913

I have received the following note from the Checoslovacian Embassy:

Consequent upon a request from the Deputy Prime Minister Bernard Coard, presented during his visit to Checoslovacia in June of 1980, the Government of Checslovacia has agreed to provide to the Government of Grenada free of cost the following items listed below:

3,000 – 7.62mm automatic rifles type: 52/57

30 boxes of spare parts (SZY 1 KU 100) for automatic rifles type 52/57

1 million cartrages for 7.62 type 43

50 bazoocas P 27

5 boxes of spare parts (SZV II) for P 27

5,000 projectiles for bazooca P 27

These pieces of equipment will be sent to Cuba between the latter part of September and the early part of October and transhipped to Grenada. We are making the necessary arrangements through the Embassy with the Ministry of the Armed Forces.

As I understand it, you have already received information about the agreement of the Government of Bulgaria to provide other military equipment.

Typed by Richard Jacobs seen also by Otto Marero

[several lines of illegible handwriting follow.]

Agreement with East Germany
10 June 1982

Agreement
on cooperation between the New JEWEL Movement of Grenada and the Socialist Unity Party of Germany for the years 1982 to 1985

Guided by the desire

to deepen the friendly relations between the New JEWEL Movement of Grenada and the Socialist Unity Party of Germany in the spirit of anti-imperialist solidarity and proletarian internationalism;

to mutually exchange information on the development of national and social liberation in Grenada and the construction of the advanced socialist society in the German Democratic Republic, and

to conduct a constant exchange of views on the international situation and the foreign policy of both Parties,

both sides agree on the following fields of cooperation for the period up to 1985:

1. The New JEWEL Movement and the Socialist Unity Party of Germany attach great importance to the mutual study of their experiences of the revolutionary struggle. Both Parties shall exchange material on the political, social, economic and cultural development of their countries.

2. The Socialist Unity Party of Germany declares its readiness to assist the New JEWEL Movement in the training and political qualification of its cadres. The Socialist Unity Party of Germany will aid the drawing up of a study programme for the acquisition of a knowledge of scientific socialism.

3. The New JEWEL Movement and the Socialist Unity Party of Germany shall exchange information of mutual interest on the development and lessons of the revolutionary process in both countries and also on international questions.

4. Both Parties proclaim their reciprocal solidarity in the struggle against imperialism and reaction and declare their readiness to promote understanding for both revolutions within the world revolutionary movement.

5. Both Parties shall promote the development of cooperation between the mass organizations of their countries.

6. The central organs of the New JEWEL Movement and the Socialist Unity Party of Germany shall enter into a mutual exchange of experiences and shall support each other in their journalistic activity.

7. Both Parties shall promote and support the development of friendly relations between the Governments and peoples of the German Democratic Republic and Grenada.

The New JEWEL Movement and the Socialist Unity Party of Germany shall further concretize these measures by means of annual working plans which shall be drawn up and agreed upon by authorized representatives of both Parties.

For the New JEWEL
Movement of Grenada

[signature]

George Louison
Member of the Political
Bureau of the Central
Committee of the New JEWEL
Movement

For the Socialist Unity
Party of Germany

[signature]

Hermann Axen
Member of the Political
Bureau and Secretary of the
Central Committee of the
Socialist Unity Party of
Germany

Berlin, 10 June 1982

Working Plan
for cooperation between the New JEWEL Movement of Grenada and
the Socialist Unity Party of Germany for the years 1982/1983

On the basis of the long-term Agreement on Cooperation between the New JEWEL Movement and the Socialist Unity Party of Germany, the following measures are laid down for the years 1982/1983:

I

The Socialist Unity Party of Germany shall receive:

1. a study delegation of the New JEWEL Movement consisting of two comrades who shall acquaint themselves with the experiences of the Socialist Unity Party of Germany.

2. in 1982 two comrades and in 1983 five comrades of the New JEWEL Movement to study at the Karl Marx party college.

3. two representatives of the New JEWEL Movement each year for a holiday visit to the German Democratic Republic.

The New JEWEL Movement of Grenada shall receive:

1. a study delegation of the Socialist Unity Party of Germany consisting of two comrades for a period of ten days to study the political work of the New JEWEL Movement in 1983.

2. in line with its wish, a temporary adviser from the Socialist Unity Party of Germany on questions of building up the Party (duration of stay to be agreed).

3. annually two representatives of the Socialist Unity Party of Germany for a holiday visit to Grenada.

Both Parties shall inform each other in good time on the dates, the subject matters and the respective representatives responsible for the fulfilment of these tasks and others which may be agreed.

III

The Socialist Unity Party of Germany shall continue to assist in the operation of the New JEWEL Movement's printing press and the training of personnel in this area.

Letter from Carames to James
(no date)

REPUBLICA DE CUBA
MINISTERIO DEL INTERIOR

Havana City

Lieutenant Colonel Liam James
Director of Security and Internal Order
Granada

Dear Comrade:

I am pleased to inform you that in compliance with the offerings of help to the security of your country, expressed by the Ambassador of the German Democratic Republic in Cuba, Harry Splinder conveyed in its occasion to the Prime Minister Maurice Bishop, the Minister of the Security of the G.D.R. has decided to give in a free way to the Security Bodies of Granada, the means and equipments that appear in the enclosed list, which, without any doubt will help to strengthen the operative capacity of the Security Bodies of your country.

These materials, which we have at hand already, will be sent to your country as soon as there is an opportunity of transportation available.

Comrade James, we hope that this modest assistance will help to strengthen the operative capacity of the Granadian Security in its struggle against the imperialism and the enemies of the country.

We do not want to say good by without stating before, the interest shown by the Comrade Ambassador of the G.D.R. to realize this assistance.

Wishing you success in your work and in the important tasks assigned to you.

Whit revolucionarity greeting,

Colonel Luis Barreiro Carames
J'Estado Mayor Central

	UNIT
1. MAGNETOPHONE	20
2. APPARATUS TO PROJECT FILM (PROYECTION MACHINE)	10
3. TYPEWRITER	15
4. IRON HELMUT	10
5. HAND COMPASS	300
6. BINOCULARS	10
7. GAS MASK	25
8. BICYCLE	32
9. COTTON UNIFORMS	500
10. UPPER SHEET	500
11. LOWER SHEET	500
12. PILLOWCASE	500
13. KNAPSACK	500
14. RAINCOAT	500
16. PISTOLS (WITH CARTRIDGES)	28
17. SANITARY BAGS	40
18. TELEPHONE "MB"	40
19. SHALE "MB"	10
20. BATTERY	200

Request for Military Assistance
7 July 1982

TELEPHONE . . .   2nd July, 1982

Revolutionary Armed Forces
Grenada

Request for Military assistance to the Peoples Revolutionary Armed Forces of Grenada from the Armed Forces of the U.S.S.R.

The present request we are asking is to conclude an agreement between the People's Revolutionary Government of Grenada and the Government of the U.S.S.R. to Arm, Feed, Clothed Equip and provide the necessary storage and study base for the consolidation and further development of the Revolutionary Armed Forces of Grenada over a period of three years.

This agreement is to take into consideration all previous assistance granted, and other existing means and facilities of the Grenada Armed Forces.

The agreement is to be reviewed on a yearly basis, at which delivery arrangements will be decided.

The plan for the development of the Armed Forces during the three (3) year period 1983 to 1985 for which the assistance is required is as follows:

1983 (i) Further consolidation of:
        (a) One Permanent Infantry Batallion.
        (b) Five (5) Reservist Infantry Batallions plus assurance and support units.
    (ii) The creation of:
        (a) Two (2) more regular Infantry Batallions
        (b) Four (4) more reservist Batallions plus assurance and support units.

1984 Formation of one additional regular Infantry Batallion, together with two (2) reservist batallions plus assurance and support units.

1985 Formation of three (3) additional reservist batallions plus assurance and support units.

The appendices (1-3) to this letter deals with the details of our request.

[4 regular Bt]
[+ 14 reservist Bt]

NJM–CPSU Agreement
27 July 1982

AGREEMENT
In cooperation between the New JEWEL Movement
of Grenada and the Communist Party
of the Soviet Union

The Central Committee of the New JEWEL Movement of Grenada
and the Central Committee Communist Party of the Soviet Union,
Guided by the desire to deepen relations between the two parties in a
spirit of friendship solidarity,
[*illeg.*] offing that common commitment to the ideals of peace, national
liberation, democracy and [*illeg.*]c socialism creates favourable opportunities for cooperation.
Proceeding from common goals in the struggle against imperialism,
neocolonialism, racialism [*illeg.*] reaction in all their forms and
manifestations,
Reasserting their constant striving to render internationalist support to
all peoples fighting for freedom, independence and social progress,
and considering that inter-party cooperation is a most important basis
for the development of [*illeg.*]y relations between the peoples of
Grenada and the Soviet Union,
have signed the present Agreement under which both parties declare
their intention:
1. Steadfastly to extend and deepen their cooperation at all levels.
2. Continuosly to exchange experience in party work and party
guidance of the social, economic and cultural development of their
countries, including regular exchange of information and materials on
the aforesaid topics.
3. Regularly to exchange delegations of party workers, to conduct
consultations and exchanges of opinion on international matters,
problems of the world revolutionary process and present-day social
development, and other matters of mutual interest.
4. To promote cooperation in the training of party and government
cadres and in furthering political competence.
5. To develop contacts between the party press and other mass
communication media, to inform the public of their countries about the

activity of the two parties, and of their home and foreign policy, and resolutely to combat hostile imperialist and reactionary propaganda.

6. To promote all-round development of inter-state relations and ties between mass organisations of their countries.

7. Periodically to coordinate and implement concrete plans of inter-party ties, including initiatives that are not covered by the present Agreement.

FOR THE NEW JEWEL   FOR THE COMMUNIST PARTY
MOVEMENT OF GRENADA   OF THE SOVIET UNION

[signature]   [signature]

Moscow, 27 July 1982

Agreement with North Korea
14 April 1983

AGREEMENT

between the People's Revolutionary Government of Grenada and the Government of the Democratic People's Republic of Korea on the free offer of military assistance to the People's Revolutionary Government of Grenada by the Democratic People's Republic of Korea.

For the purposes of further cementing and developing the friendship and solidarity between the peoples and armies of the two countries established in the common struggle to oppose against imperialism, consolidate the national sovereignty and safeguard independence, and strengthening the national defence power of Grenada, the People's Revolutionary Government of the Democratic People's Republic of Korea have agreed as follows;

Article 1

The Government of the Democratic People's Republic of Korea

shall give, in 1983–1984, the free military assistance subject to weapons and ammunitions covering
US $12,000,000 indicated in Annex to this Agreement.

Article 2

The Grenadian side shall be responsible for the transport of weapons and ammunitions to be rendered to the People's Revolutionary Government of Grenada by the Democratic People's Republic of Korea.

Article

Both sides shall strictly keep the secrecy of the military assistance to be executed according to this Agreement and have an obligation not to hand over any matters of this Agreement to the third country.

Article 4

This Agreement shall come into force on the day of its signing.

This Agreement has been prepared in duplicate in the Korean and English languages and signed in Pyongyang on April 14, 1983, two original equally authentic.

[signature]   [signature]

By the authority of the   By the authority of the
People's Revolutionary   Government of the
Government of Grenada.   Democratic People's
                                                        Republic of Korea.

ANNEX
of Agreement on the free offer of military assistance to the People's Revolutionary Government of Grenada by the Democratic People's Republic of Korea.

Hand flares	200 pcs
Ammunition for hand flares	4,000 rds
7.62mm automatic rifle	1,000 pcs
7.62mm light machine gun	50 pcs
Ammunition for 7.62mm auto. rifle	360,000 rds
7.62mm blanks	300,000 rds
7.62mm heavy machine gun	30 pcs
Ammunition for heavy machine gun	60,000 rds
RPG-7 launcher	50 pcs
RPG-7	500 rds
Hand grenade	200 rds
Instruction hand grenade	20 rds
Binoculars (8×)	30 pcs
Anti-gas masks	1,000 pcs
Sirens	50 pcs
Tactical drawing instruments	15 sets
Coast guard	2 boats
Uniforms	6,000 suits
Knapsacks	6,000 pcs
Camouflage nets	50 pcs
Ultrashort waves wireless set (= -3)	3 pcs
Ultrashort waves wireless set (= -4)	3 pcs

2. TRAINING AND CO-OPERATION

Letter from Bishop to Ortega
17 July 1981

[*17.7.81*]

TO: COMMANDANTE DANIEL ORTEGA SAAVEDRA
COMMANDER OF THE NICARAGUAN
REVOLUTION.

[*My dear Daniel*]

Warmest fraternal and Revolutionary greetings!

On the occasion of the second Anniversary of the glorious Nicaraguan Revolution Our Party, Government and People extend our total and complete solidarity with the FSLN, your Government of National Reconstruction and the fighting children of Sandino.

---

*Comandante (corrected spelling) Daniel Ortega Saavedra, born on 11 November 1945, joined the Nicaraguan Patriotic Youth when he was 15 and was active against the Somoza regime during the next few years. In 1967 he was gaoled for seven years for taking part in a bank robbery. He joined the Sandinista National Liberation Front (Frente Sandinista de Liberación Nacional, named after General Augusto C. Sandino, who had opposed the American occupation of Nicaragua in the 1920s and 1930s and was later assassinated on orders from President Anastasio Somoza's father). After a guerrilla campaign masterminded by Cuba, the Sandinistas overthrew the Somoza dictatorship and entered Managua on 19 July 1979. Ortega emerged as a member of the Sandinista Junta de Reconstruccion Nacional and was made Co-ordinator in 1981. He has been President of the Republic since January 1985.

Cde Hudson Austin, Member of our Political Bureau and General of the People's Revolutionary Army, will be representing our Party and Government at your second Anniversary. Cde Austin will be very anxious to discuss the present situation in Nicaragua and to inform you of our present situation. I am certain, from the reports we have been receiving, that our two situations are under similar pressures. It is clear that U.S. Imperialism has decided to make an all-out onslaught on our two Revolutions. The propaganda war, the economic aggression, the Political and Industrial destabilisation and the threat of mercenary invasion all lead to the unmistakeable conclusion that imperialism has decided to attempt to overthrow our popular Revolutions this year. That is their decision; but we have made our own decision that our Revolutions will continue and undoubtedly we will win out. As our People say in Grenada—A UNITED, CONSCIOUS, ORGANISED AND VIGILANT PEOPLE CAN NEVER BE DEFEATED.

In whatever way we can, and at whatever cost, the Grenada Revolution and the People of Grenada will always stand with the Nicaraguan Revolution and the People of Nicaragua.

LONG LIVE THE NICARAGUAN REVOLUTION:

LONG LIVE THE FSLN!

LONG LIVE THE UNBREAKABLE BONDS OF FRIEND-SHIP BETWEEN THE PEOPLE OF GRENADA AND NICARAGUA!

FORWARD EVER, BACKWARD NEVER!

A Warm Embrace,

[*Maurice*]

Letter from Austin to Andropov
17 February 1982

MINISTRY OF INTERIOR

[BUTLER HOUSE]
ST. GEORGE'S
[GRENADA]
WEST INDIES

TEL: 3383 3020   17th Feb 1982

TO: Commander Andropov
         Chairman of the Committee of State Security
         Member of Politiburo

FROM: General of the Army Hudson Austin

Dear Comrade,

Warmest revolutionary greetings to you, the Communist Party of Soviet Union and all Soviet people, from the Political Bureau of the New Jewel Movement, Government, Armed Forces and all the Grenadian people.

Let me first of all extend our deepest sympathies to your Party and people on the passing away of comrade Suslov, a true Bolshevik and hero of revolutionary people worldwide.

---

*Strictly speaking, Austin's letter should have been addressed to General (not Commander) Yuriy V. (Vladimirovich) Andropov. Nine months later, in November 1982, Andropov succeeded Leonid Brezhnev, recently deceased, as General Secretary of the ruling Communist Party of the Soviet Union (CPSU). Hudson Austin played a leading part both in the 1979 bloodless coup which brought Maurice Bishop to power, and in the 1985 coup which removed the latter. He first met Bishop while on guard duty at the gaol where Bishop was a political prisoner. His grandiose title of 'General of the Army' referred to his post as commander of Grenada's tiny army and militia. After the anti-Bishop coup Austin headed the sixteen-member council he had helped to bring to power.

[*I write at this time to*] request assistance in the strengthening of our Ministry of Interior. This request stems from discussions [*held between*] Cde. Vladmir Klimentov, then attached to the Soviet Embassy in Jamaica, [*illeg.*] Comrade Maurice Bishop, Chairman of the Central Committee of our Party the New Jewel Movement, Prime Minister and Minister of Defence and Interior of the People's Revolutionary Government, Comrade Liam James, Member of the Central Committee of our Party and Head of the Ministry of Interior [*and myself. Peoples Revo. Govt.* illeg. *formally request the following*] training courses for four (4) [*of our*] comrades:-

a) Basic course in Counter Intelligence for the period of one (1) year— three (3) comrades

b) Basic course in Intelligence for a period of one (1) year—one (1) comrade.

We thank you once again for the tremendous assistance which our Armed Forces have received from your Party and Government in the past. We recognise the tremendous internationalist obligations of your people, yet we sincerely hope that these courses will be made available to our comrades in 1982, given the pressing needs in our Ministry and the continuing threat being posted to the Grenada Revolution by United States Imperialism.

I close by once again extending our greatest warmth and embrace to you and your Party—Sons and Daughters of the heroic Lenin. I look forward to hearing from you soon.

Yours Fraternally,

. . . .
General Hudson Austin
Member of the Political Bureau of NJM
Secretary of Defence and Interior

Letter from Bishop to Ustinov
17 February 1982

MINISTRY OF DEFENCE

FORT RUPERT   ST. GEORGE'S
GRENADA   WEST INDIES

TELEPHONE: 2263 2378   17th February 1982

TO: MARSHAL DIMITROV USTINOV,*
      MINISTER OF DEFENCE
      USSR

FROM: MINISTER OF DEFENCE, MAURICE BISHOP.

Dear Comrade,

Revolutionary greetings to you, the Communist Party of the Soviet Union and all Soviet people, from the Political Bureau of the New Jewel Movement, Government, Armed Forces and all the Grenadian people.

I am writing this letter to you in reference to training for personnel of the Grenadian Armed Forces in your country.

Based on Article Three of the Signed Protocol between the Government of Grenada and the Government of the USSR of 27th October, 1980 in Havana, Cuba, I hereby make the following request—

---

*The addressee was, of course, Marshal Dimitriy (not 'Dimitrov') Ustinov. Maurice Bishop's more exalted titles are given after his signature, although he wrote in his capacity of Minister of Defence. Born in 1944 at Aruba in the Netherlands Antilles, in a prosperous family of hoteliers, Bishop read law in London where he was called to the Bar in 1966. Back in Grenada four years later he practised in partnership with the man who would later have him ousted in the 1983 coup in which he lost his life, Bernard Coard. Elected to Parliament in 1976, Bishop was one of the original leaders of the Marxist–Leninist New Jewel Movement (NJM).

1. Military preparation for twenty (20) Junior Officers in the following areas in courses lasting a period of one year;

a)	General Troops	— 6
b)	Exploration	— 3
c)	Communication	— 2
d)	Engineering	— 2
e)	Logistics	— 3
f)	Anti-Aircraft Artillery	— 2
g)	Terrestrial	— 2

2. Training for five (5) senior officers of the General Staff of the armed forces on a rotational basis in courses lasting three to six months.

The comrades who will be prepared in these courses are the leaders of our armed forces and as such cannot stay away for long periods at this time.

The areas of preparation for the comrades will be—

a) General Troops — 4
b) Political work in the Armed Forces — 1

We are hopeful that these courses will commence in 1982 and as such we are commencing all the preliminary work for the departure of our comrades.

Comrade Marshal, I want to thank you once more for all the assistance our armed forces have received from your country and say that we are extremely thankful for that.

Finally, I want to say that our Party and Armed Forces look forward with the greatest expectations to our comrades receiving training with the glorious Red Army, in the land of the Immortal Lenin and the Great October Revolution which opened a new world to mankind.

We thank you in advance for your kind co-operation and look forward to hearing from you soon.

Maurice Bishop,
COMMANDER IN CHIEF,
CHAIRMAN OF THE CENTRAL COMMITTEE
OF NJM,
PRIME MINISTER AND MINISTER OF
DEFENCE AND INTERIOR.

Co-operation Agreement between Cuba and Grenada
29 June 1983

TOP SECRET

PARTIDO COMUNISTA DE CUBA/COMITE CENTRAL

SECRET

COOPERATION AND EXCHANGE OF PLAN BETWEEN THE COMMUNIST PARTY OF CUBA AND THE NEW JEWEL MOVEMENT OF GRENADA, FOR THE 1983 PERIOD

INTRODUCTION

The Communist Party of Cuba and the New Jewel Movement, brotherly united by the same ideals of struggle in their respective countries, as well as of active solidarity in favor of the peoples that struggle for national liberation, and likewise, sharing the same convictions against imperialism, colonialism, neocolonialism, Zionism, and racism, become aware of the need to unite efforts and coordinate actions of cooperation in the different activities within their scope.

. . . .

Both Parties, on agreeing that the many-sided relations of cooperation be governed by the widest and justest spirit of cooperation, solidarity, and internationalism, reach agreement on the following:

b) The CPC expresses its willingness to send, according to the requests formulated by the NJM in this sense, technical advisers for the organization of public meetings and propaganda of the Party in Grenada.

c) Regarding the political upgrading and professional assistance, the NJM and the CPC express their willingness to receive, at the "Nico Lopez" School, the NJM cadres that will be decided on mutual agreement.

d) The CPC and the NJM of Grenada will exchange information of mutual interest, both on the field of the development of the two revolutions and their experiences, as well as on the international situation and, fundamentally, that of the Caribbean in its struggle against imperialism, neocolonialism, racism and Zionism. Like-wise, they will exchange information on the liberation movements as well as coordinate actions and positions of mutual interest to be adopted at events, conferences, and other Party activities of an international character, with special emphasis on the problems in the Caribbean.

. . . .

The CPC and the NJM will coordinate the positions of the governments of Cuba and Grenada at international events, conferences, and agencies where they participate, in attention to the political, economic and social interests of both Parties.

. . . .

The Communist Party of Cuba and the New Jewel Movement of Grenada, satisfied by the discussed and agreed aspects, which fully correspond with the fraternal relations between both Parties, under-write this document in the City of Havana, Cuba, June 29th, 1983.

[signature]   [signature]
The Communist Party   The New Jewel
   of Cuba   Movement

Letter from Bishop to Assad
4 October 1979

4th October, 1979

H.E. Hafez El Assad,
President of the Arab Republic of Syria,*
Arab Republic of Syria,
C/O The U.N. Ambassador from Syria,
Syrian Embassy,
New York,
U.S.A.

I am very happy to take this opportunity to write to you concerning the discussions we recently had in Havana during the Non-Aligned Conference.

You will recall that during our discussions, we agreed on the need for our countries to establish diplomatic relations at the earliest opportunity and thereafter for your country to accredit your Ambassador to Havana to Grenada.

We also agreed that a Technical Co-operation Team from your country should visit Grenada at an early opportunity with a view to assessing areas of possible technical and economic co-operation and assistance between our countries. Needless to say, I am very anxious for further discussion on these areas of possible co-operation and as such, on behalf of the People's Revolutionary Government of Grenada and the people of Grenada, I am inviting you to send such a team to Grenada as soon as possible.

I want you to know that it was a real pleasure for me to have had the opportunity to discuss so many matters of mutual concern to our countries with you. I sincerely hope that you will be able to come to our

---

*Strictly speaking, Syria is a client-State of the Soviet Union, as distinct from such *satellites* as Cuba, Bulgaria or East Germany (the German Democratic Republic or GDR) with which the New Jewel Movement regime established close and co-operative relations. On 8 October 1980 in Moscow, President Hafez Assad of Syria and President Brezhnev of the USSR signed a Treaty of Friendship and Co-operation, the terms of which amounted to a quasi-alliance.

country on a state visit at a mutually convenient date in the future. At the same time, until that visit, I am asking you to assist our people in Grenada to learn more about The Republic of Syria and as such we would very much appreciate receiving, if possible, copies of any radio tapes, television video tapes, 16mm or 35mm films or printed matter that your government may have on your country and your struggle for true independence.

We would also welcome a visit to our country by any cultural group from your country that might happen to be coming to this region.

You can rest assured of the continued support of our government and party to the just cause of the Palestinians under the leadership of the P.L.O., our commitment to continue resisting the manoeuvrings of imperialism and the Israeli Zionists and our continued opposition to the treacherous Camp David Agreement.

On behalf of my government, party and people I send warmest fraternal regards to you, your government and people.

Long live the just struggle of the Arab Republic of Syria for social progress, genuine independence and peace with justice in the Middle East!

Yours fraternally

. . . .
MAURICE BISHOP,
PRIME MINISTER.

3. IDEOLOGY, PROPAGANDA AND SECURITY

The documents in this section provide concrete evidence of plans (rapidly implemented) to turn Grenada under the New Jewel Movement into a typically totalitarian Marxist–Leninist police State.

General Intelligence Operations

Although undated, this brief report presumably was issued shortly after the 1979 coup which brought Maurice Bishop and his NJM to power. It provides for the monitoring of all diplomatic missions and visitors to the island republic. Students and teachers at the Medical School are also to be monitored, as well as the churches. As elsewhere, spellings (e.g. 'hirachy') have been left as in the original. 'Counters' stands for 'counter-revolutionaries'.

MINISTRY OF INTERIOR
BUTLER HOUSE,
ST. GEORGE'S.

PLAN OF G.I. [General Intelligence] OPERATIONS

Setting up of command post comprising Major Keith Roberts, Cpt. H. Romain, Lt. B. Pivotta.

Responsible for analyzing all information that are coming in, in order to pass on to members of the Central Committee.

47

— Also, one Comrade who we can send to verify situations and incidents that have been reported.

— Recorder of all the information coming into the Centre.

MONITORING REGIONALLY—ST. GEORGE'S

City—three (3) Officers
Dock, Carenage—one (1) Officer
St. Paul's—two (2) Officers

ST. JOHN'S

One (1) Officer plus Party Cadres—Valdon

ST. PATRICK'S

(R)eports from Jan

T. ANDREW'S

Two (2) Officers plus Party Cadres—Re Gill
Regular hourly report from all officers and Party Cadres being [*illeg.*]ed for this purpose.

(i)   Monitoring of all Embassies and Diplomats in this period.

(ii)   To control the movements of all diplomats, with the purpose of revealing the links with possible counter elements.

(iii)   Stop any possibility of them actively using this period to create disturbances and confusion and a major counter-action.

(iv)   Study the incoming visitors of the various counters to see the composition of visitors.

(vi)   Checking and controlling the key middle class elements who have links with diplomats and influence in some section of the society.

(vii)   Check the hotels to see if visitors are leaving before their scheduled time or the booking question.

MEDICAL SCHOOL

Monitor all students during this period.
Check the mood and movements of the school hirachy and professors during this period.

CHURCH

Monitor all sermons by the various parish priests and preachers in the society.
The controlling of all hirachy meeting of the church in particular the Catholic and Anglicans.
Controlling all elements of the society that pay visits to the Hirachy.
Tapping of the Hirachy of all the leading counter churches phones.

ESSENTIAL SERVICES

[*illeg.*] protection of the key installations against sabotage. [*illeg.*] on confidence people to ensure that any signs of [*illeg.*] may be identified.
Getting a general operative picture of the area in which the key installations are located.
Checking of mails of dangerous elements.
Tapping and disconnection of dangerous elements phones.
Check all Heads of Ministries to see if they have any important documents which needs to be secured.
Special control over technicians who are not very firm and cannot be replaced.

COAST GUARD

Establish communication with watch towers.
Boat patrols on a nightly basis.

Documentation of all telephone calls and security reports from various regions.

Propaganda Work-Plan

This Report, much more extensive than the previous one, is likewise undated. It is a typically Leninist document, designed to ensure that the Party line, with its 'anti-imperialist' slant, is constantly disseminated through all possible outlets. It should be noted that under OBJECTIVE 7 (deepening the internationalist spirit, etc.), the 'ways and means' stipulated include the distribution of 'progressive materials' from the Soviet Union, 'other Socialist countries and progressive parties'.

WORK-PLAN OF THE PARTY'S PROPAGANDA DEPARTMENT

I. OBJECTIVE: Organise propaganda campaigns around important events and activities of the party.

WAYS AND MEANS:

(i)   Identify key events and activities of the party for 1983.

(ii)   Develop work plans and schedules for specific events and activities.

OBJECTIVE 2: Lift the political, academic and ideological levels of the masses.

WAYS AND MEANS:

(i)   ENCOURAGE participations in the CPE programme, Worker education classes and the work-study programme.

(ii)   Recommence publication of all the leading Party Organs.

(iii) Publish theoretical articles in all Party publications.

OBJECTIVE 3: Coordinate the publication and distribution of all Party Organs.

WAYS AND MEANS:

(i)   Prepare articles in conjunction with the editors of the respective organs.

(ii) Hold regular meetings with the editorial committees of the respective organs to review strength and weaknesses.

(iii) Set up a central distribution system.

OBJECTIVE 4: Document all speeches and publications of the party and leadership.

WAYS AND MEANS:

(i)   Tape edit and reproduce major speeches of Party members.

(ii) File all publications and other documents of the Party.

OBJECTIVE 5: ENSURE press coverage of all public party activities.

WAYS AND MEANS:

(i)   Obtain a list of party activities every month.

(ii) Co-ordinate with SPEC—attend the weekly meetings.

OBJECTIVE 6: Deepen the consciousness of the masses as to the history and vanguard role of the party and the heroes of the revolution.

WAYS AND MEANS:

(i)   Research, document and publish information on the heroes of the revolution.

(ii) Prepare booklet on the history of the party—10 years.

(iii) Prepare materials on specific historic events of the party— peoples congress etc.

(iv)   Provide general information on the party and its leadership (profiles etc.).

OBJECTIVE 7: Deepen the internationalist spirit and socialist consciousness of the Grenadian masses.

WAYS AND MEANS:

(i)   Distribute progressive materials received from the Soviet Union other Socialist countries and progressive parties.

(ii)   Highlight the struggles of National Liberation Movements.

(iii)   Highlight the struggles of other countries against imperialism.

(iv)   Highlight the immense benefits to workers under socialism.

(v)   Expose the evil and warmongering policies of imperialism.

(vi)   Highlight the struggles of the working class under capitalism.

(vii)   Promote the life of people under socialism.

OBJECTIVE 8: Deepen the Patriotic [word missing] of the masses and cultivate even stronger desires to participate in National defence.

WAYS AND MEANS:

(i)   Highlight activities of the people Revolutionary Armed Forces (PRAF).

(ii)   constantly expose the [word missing] of imperialism towards the Grenada Revolution.

(iii)   Consistently highlight the critical importance of National Defense.

(iv)   Highlight the message to be delivered by soldier of the PRAF.

(v) Propagandise the new programme of technical and academic training in the PRAF.

OBJECTIVE 9: Encourage the masses to actively participate in economic construction and stress the need to constantly lift the levels of production and productivity.

WAYS AND MEANS:

(i) Develop specific programs around the National budget and plan.

(ii) Extensive promotion of the emulation programme in the different party publications.

(iii) Constantly remind the masses of the economic problems inherited by the revolution and the pressures of imperialism.

(iv) Highlight the numerous economic projects of the revolution.

(v) Promote the views of workers on ways to lift production and productivity.

OBJECTIVE 10: Defend the party and revolution against counter revolutionary, backward and reactionary attacks from inside and outside of Grenada.

(i) Respond to all attacks against the party and revolution.

(ii) Consistently promote the achievements of the revolution in all areas.

OBJECTIVE 11: Ensure that fraternal parties—regionally and internationally—receives news, speeches and other documents of the party.

WAYS AND MEANS:

(i) Obtain names and addresses of all progressive and revolutionary parties in the region.

(ii)   Regularly send out news, speeches and other documents of the party.

OBJECTIVE 12: Deepen the awareness and strengthen the resolve of Grenadians to struggle for World Peace, detente and disarmament.

WAYS AND MEANS:

(i)   Highlight the activities of the peace movements around the world.

(ii)   Promote the effects of the party and revolution on the question of world peace and for the Caribbean to be declared a zone of peace.

(iii) Publicise the activities of the socialist and democratic world for peace, disarmament and detente.

OBJECTIVE 13: guide and co-ordinate the propaganda of the mass organisations and other party bodies.

(i)   Regular meetings with propaganda representatives and leadership of Party Committees.

(ii)   Assist in drawing up propaganda plans for the different bodies.

RADIO AND TV PROPAGANDA

(1) Interviews
(2) News
(3) Special Programmes
(4) Promos
(5) Music
(6) Announcements
(7) Poetry
(8) Extracts from Speeches

ASPECTS OF PROPAGANDA

(1) Newspapers
(2) Pamphlets
(3) Bill-boards
(4) Badges
(5) Leadership speeches
(6) Radio and Television
(7) Posters
(8) Statements
(9) Jerseys and Pens
(10) Photography/Cartoons
(11) Letters to the Editor
(12) Photographic Exhibitions
(13) Newspaper displays reflecting the role of the party
(14) Use of Public Address Systems
(15) Use of Almanacs
(16) Booklets
(17) Photo stories
(18) Use of films and videos

PARTY PUBLICATIONS

(1) New Jewel — N.J.M.
(2) Fight — N.Y.O.
(3) The Scotilda — N.W.O.
(4) Cutlass — A.G.W.U.
(5) Fork — P.F.U.
(6) Pioneers Voice — N.F.M.
(7) Workers Voice — W.C.
(8) Fedon — P.R.A.F.

Course Content: The concept of "Class Struggle" was taught for the second time.

SOME QUESTIONS AND ANSWERS:

TUTOR: In order to fully grasp the essence of Class Struggle in our present society it is important to fully understand the class struggle between the slaves and the slaves masters.

TUTOR: How many classes existed in the slave society?

MASS PARTICIPATION: Two main classes—Slaves/Slave Owners

George Best: Slaves lived under very bad conditions.

TUTOR: What are these bad conditions?

Victor Julien: No freedom of speech.

Anthony Lewis: Forced Labour for no wages.

Dollis McKenzie: Slaves were compelled to work without choice.

Jacqueline Charles: Poor housing facilities.

Leroy John: Slaves were made to work 24 hours without food or very little food.

Cleaver Williams: Harsh penalties for resisting work/poor medical care.

Antoinette Martin: Slaves owned nothing not even themselves.

TUTOR: Why do you think that the class of slave masters put the slaves under these kind of conditions?

Keith Jeremiah: They did this in order to maintain their slave system.

Terence McPhail: The whole system is geared to benefit one class. All the benefit goes to the slave master.

Nola Nelson: Because he can make much more for himself.

TUTOR: Did slavery remain forever?

Mass participation: No! slaves rebelled, slavery lasted for over 400 years.

TUTOR: We agree that in Modern Capitalist society there are two main classes—Capitalist/Working class.

Is there class struggle under Capitalism?

Mass participation: Yes—the struggle between the capitalist and the workers.

TUTOR: Why is there class struggle under capitalist capitalism?

Mass Participation: It is the interest of the capitalist to take the lion share of what is produced and give the workers less.

TUTOR: More for the capitalist means less for the workers and less for the capitalist means more for the workers.

TUTOR: Do you think it is fair for the capitalist to get the lion share?

Wharwood: Workers use their strength to create the wealth—they should get the biggest share.

Soniania Frederick: We should get a good share but not the lion share.

Anthony Lewis/Ambrose Smith: Capitalist owns the means—workers own the labour.

Sharon De Bourg: [missing word] power so profits should be equally divided.

Dollis McKenzie: If the capitalist did not buy the machinery, the workers could not work, so worker should not get the biggest share but a reasonable share.

TUTOR: The most important thing here is to show that class struggle arose as result of exploitations of one class by another class.

TUTOR: What is the main objective of the exploiter class?

TUTOR: How does the capitalist make more profits.

Anthony Lewis: Cheaper Labour.

Leroy John: Longer working hours.

George Best: Increase in prices.

Errol Antoine: Cutting staff (more work for workers—less wages paid out)

Anthony Lewis: non recognition of Trade Unions.

TUTOR: If workers don't struggle—what will happen to their share of the cake.

Mass participation: It will get sam a smaller.

TUTOR: 1. It is important to understand, that to struggle is a necessity—struggle leads to progress.

2. In a class society, there is always class struggle.

3. Class struggle is the engine of progress.

Anthony Lewis: Is there class on a universal scale?
Is there class struggle in the U.S.S.R.?

TUTOR: In response to the above questions, tutors started that these questions will be looked at in the next session.

At this state a short address was delivered by A.U.C.C.T.U. Representative Bro. Boris Pirchgun who focussed on these two areas. 1. Class in the U.S.S.R. 2. Korean Airline.

ANALYSIS: Overall the participation was very good. From a scale of 0.5 participation can be rated as 3.5. Generally the mood of the workers was good.

Youth Meetings in Moscow

These undated notes refer to meetings between the National Youth Organisation (NYO) of the NJM with the Soviet Komsomol (Youth League of the Communist Party of the Soviet Union) on the occasion of the Komsomol Congress in May 1982. The then leader of the NYO, Leon Cornwall, led the Grenadian delegation, and the notes were prepared by the NYO Chairman David Tan Bartholomew. They reveal an overall plan for Grenadian youth indoctrination on the Soviet model.

ISSUES FOR DISCUSSION BETWEEN LENINIST KOMSOMOL AND THE NEW JEWEL MOVEMENT- NATIONAL YOUTH ORGANISATION NJM-NYO

The former Leader of the New jewel Movement—National Youth Organisation (NJM-NYO), comrade Leon Cornwall, held discussions with Leninist Komsomol during his visit to the Soviet Union to attend the Komsomol Congress in May 1982. The discussions centered on, among other things, the question of desperately needed material assistance to NYO. This Delegation has the responsibility of following up on discussions held between Comrade Cornwall and the Leninist Komsomol.

THE FOLLOWING WERE DISCUSSED BETWEEN KOMSOMOL AND NYO

1. Leninist Komsomol agreed to receive a four (4) man Delegation from NYO in November, to further study Y.C.L. activities. This presant NYO Delegation is the fulfilment of this agreement. We attach tremendous significance and importance to this visit, because we think we can learn from the tremendous experience accumulated by the Komsomol, which we may be able to creatively apply to our local situation.

2. Leninist Komsomol offered a Scholarship to one (1) Grenadian Youth to study an academic subject in the USSR for three (3) years. NYO now proposed that the area of study be Journalism given the importance of this area to us and the unavailability of this skill. Our

propaganda work is seriously affected by the absence of comrades with skill in Journalism.

3. Leninist Komsomol had invited two (2) Pioneers and a Guide to attend a Pioneer Camp, in USSR in July 1982, this took place. The experience and knowledge gained during the Camp has helped our young comrades in their work at Home.

4. Leninist Komsomol had proposed for consideration a friendship festival with NYO with all expenses to be paid by Komsomol. The proposal was that two (2) festivals one (1) 1983 in Grenada and two (2) 1985 in Soviet Union. NYO now proposes a rescheduling of the festival to 1984 in Grenada and 1985 in USSR.

5. Komsomol agreed to assist NYO with Sporting equipment, Camera, Loud Speakers and Marxist-Leninist literature. We have already received Literature earlier this year from Komsomol. This is being used as part of the NYO Library where comrades can borrow books to be used for ideological study. The thirst for Marxist-Leninist ideas is very intense among our Youth, we are unfortunately far from being able to satisfy this positive demand. However, the most important thing for the NYO at this point in time is Sporting equipment Our Youth are sport fanatic. Sport remain and will remain for a long time the main vehicle around which we can mobilise and organise our youth. Unemployment is one of the main social and economic problems facing Grenada. The rate of unemployed people are between 10% of the work force. But 65% of all unemployed people are between the ages of 16-25 years. This large reserve Army of unemployed youths are turning to drugs to ease frustration. We are concerned that opportunist, bourgeois elements in alliance with imperialism will use the frustrated youth against the Revolution.

In 1980 left-opportunist were able to organise a section of the unemployed youth against the Revolution. This was firmly crushed, but the unemployed youth has remain a potential reserve for Reactionary activities. Sport is the vehicle through which we can mobilise and organise these youths and divert them from the negitave tendancies. The organisation of sport is our number one strategic priority. We will provide a list of the specific equipment we need desperately.

6. Komsomol had promised also to look into the possibility of giving assistance with clothing for the Youth Agricultural Training Schools. These schools are organised by the Ministry of Agriculture and NYO where unemployed youth live in Schools set up to teach new methods of Agriculture.

7. Komsomol had also promised to investigate the possibility of assisting NYO with two (2) Jeeps. Our second most crucial problem is Transportation. Our youths are organised in hundreds of base groups throughout the Country. These Groups cannot be serviced effectively without Transport. We will appreciate greatly assistance in this area.

8. Komsomol also promised to contact us on the possibility of giving ideological training to youths in USSR or to send a lecturer down to Grenada for a week or two.

NEW PROPOSALS

1. Assistance with (a) films and Projectors (b) Typewriters.

Film/Projectors

   Ideological education is presantly one of the main priorities of our Party. Experience have proved beyond doubt that the most effective methods of ideological education for our Mass Organisations is through Film Shows. Assistance in this field will greatly enhance our ideological work among youth and students.

Typewriters

   Our administration department suffers from the shortage of type writers. With the expansion of our work the administrative department will also have to be expanded. Assistance with typewriters will help us tremendously.

   The assistance requested will help our organisation to solve serious objective problems that has been holding back the development of our work. We are convinced that assistance requested could qualitatively improve our work among the Grenadian youth and student thereby preparing them to play a major role in building the new Society.

Comradely,

[signature]

DAVE TAN BARTHOLOMEW
CHAIRMAN—NJM—NATIONAL
YOUTH ORGANISATION

4. SOVIET-BLOC ACTIVITIES

This section complements the earlier sections on TREATIES WITH SOVIET-BLOC COUNTRIES, TRAINING AND CO-OPERATION, and IDEOLOGY, PROPAGANDA AND SECURITY. They show the extent to which Grenada, in a comparatively brief time, had become integrated with the Soviet empire.

Meeting of Soviet and Grenadian
Military Chiefs of Staff
10 March 1983

There is a certain incongruity in a meeting between a major of the miniscule 'People's Revolutionary Armed Forces of Grenada' and the military leader of the communist superpower, the then Chief of Staff of the Soviet Armed Forces, Marshal of the Soviet Union Nikolai V. Ogarkov, with some of his advisers. The Grenadian participant, Major Einstein Louison, used the opportunity to remind the Soviet side that in July of the previous year, 1982, the NJM government had requested additional Soviet assistance especially in food, fuel and spare parts, which had not yet been delivered at the time of the meeting (10 March 1983), Ogarkov promised that 'all items contained in the protocol would be delivered'. In a revealing passage, Ogarkov threw light on Soviet expansionism in the Caribbean region: 'Over two decades ago, there was only Cuba in Latin America, today there are Nicaragua, Grenada, and a serious battle is going on in El Salvador.'

EMBASSY OF GRENADA IN THE USER

Dobryninskaya Ulitsa 7 *Telephone*
Apartment 221 *237–25–41*
Moscow *237–99–05*
USSR

MEETING BETWEEN CHIEFS OF GENERAL STAFF OF SOVIET ARMED FORCES AND PEOPLE'S REVOLUTIONARY ARMED FORCES OF GRENADA

DATE: THURSDAY 10 MARCH 1983 (4.00 pm)

Representing the Soviet side were:
1. Marshal of the Soviet Union Ogarkov N.V. Chief of Staff
2. Colonel General N.A. Zutov 10th Department
3. Lt.-General G.A. Borisov Foreign relations Department
4. Colonel Soloviev 10th Department
5. Captain M. Globenko Foreign Relations Department

Present on the Grenada side were:
1. Major Einstein Louison Chief of Staff
2. Bernard Bourne Minister-Counsellor

The meeting commenced promptly by Marshal Ogarkov who extended a warm welcome to Major Louison. In doing so, Marshal Ogarkov enquired whether Major Louison was having any problems with his studies and living conditions.

Major Louison expressed thanks for the words of welcome and explained that he had no difficulty with studies and thought that he was making progress because there was no report to the contrary from the professors at the school.

Speaking about the Grenada Revolution Major Louison pointed out that the economy had grown by 5.5% (percent) in 1982 and living standards by 3 percent. He explained that the United States continues with its plans to destabilize the revolution, undermine tourism, linking our international airport with military potential and training of mercenaries in Venezuela, in addition to the United States itself. Major Louison then emphasized that the Granada Revolution got around these problems and still continued to make advances. He also informed Marshal Ogarkov that at the Seventh Non-Aligned Summit Grenada was again elected to the coordinating Bureau of the Movement.

At the moment Marshal Ogarkov said that he was glad for the information on Grenada. About the situation in the world Marshal Ogarkov pointed out that the United States would try now and in the future to make things difficult for progressive changes in all regions and continents. The Marshal said that over two decades ago, there was only Cuba in Latin America, today there are Nicaragua, Grenada and a serious battle is going on in El Salvador. The Marshal of the Soviet Union then stressed that United States imperialism would try to prevent progress but that there were no prospects for imperialism to turn back history.

Moreover, Marshal Ogarkov emphasized that in an aggressive climate the military people have tasks to do. He explained that since Grenada was located close to US imperialism and was not developed militarily the Grenada Revolution would have to be specifically vigilant at all times. Furthermore, the Marshal declared that once the masses have a burning desire for progress the leadership should move ahead decisively and firmly. On the point Marshal Ogarkov assured Major Louison that the plans outlined by Prime Minister Maurice Bishop during his visit to the Soviet Union in 1982 were good and had the support of the Grenadian people.

Further still, the Marshal of the Soviet Union reminded Major Louison that the Soviet Union would contribute to raising the combat readiness and preparedness of the Armed Forces of Grenada.

He informed the Grenada Chief of Staff that according to the agreement signed in July 1982, one-third of the means for 1983 were already supplied and the rest would be delivered during this year.

In response Major Louison expressed his gratitude for the supplies sent to Grenada and mentioned that he was confident that more deliveries would be sent to Grenada in the future.

However, Major Louison explained that he wished to introduce another matter for discussion which was not included in the protocol. The Chief of Staff of Grenada explained that he was referring to the text of a letter from Prime Minister Bishop addressed to Prime Minister Tikhonov dated 28th July 1982. Major Louison said that in the letter, Grenada was requesting additional assistance in: food, fuel, spare parts, transportation, engineering kits, uniforms and others. He disclosed that the greatest part of the budget was used for food and fuel and that spare parts were also of serious concern because many vehicles were grounded since the basic spare parts were unavailable.

Marshal Ogarkov replied rather jokingly that students should be concerned with studies, but that Major Louison who would graduate on 10th May was also concerned about the problems of his soldiers. Nevertheless, the Marshal indicated that he was aware of such requests, but hastened to assure Major Louison that all items contained in the protocol would be delivered. Marshal Ogarkov further assured Major Louison that the requests contained in the letter to P.M. Tikhonov were presently under consideration and that even though they were handled by GKS and Ministry of Foreign Trade, the Ministry of Defence would exercise some control on the solution. He said, with confidence, that his Ministry would participate in the settlement of these requests.

Further still, the Marshal disclosed that there was a possibility that some of the main questions would be solved and as soon as a decision was taken, the Ministry of Defence through Col-General Zutov would inform the Embassy.

Additionally, referring to the question of deputation of Soviet specialists to Grenada to conduct studies related to the construction of military projects the Marshal informed the Grenadian side that the team of specialists would be sent in one month's time and that they await an indication from Grenada confirming readiness to accommodate the specialists.

Finally, towards the end of the meeting the Marshal of the Soviet Union and Chief of Staff of the Soviet Armed Forces proposed a toast 'from the bottom of our hearts'—in his words—to Major Louison on the eve of the 10th Anniversary of the New JEWEL Movement and the fourth Anniversary of the Grenada Revolution.

In his turn, Major Louison expressed thanks and appreciation to the Marshal for the kind words about the Grenada Revolution; Major Louison also expressed thanks for the assistance to the Armed Forces of Grenada and then raised a toast towards the strengthening of relations between the two countries, parties, people's, and their armed forces.

Marshal Ogarkov was thankful for the warm meeting and reinforced both toasts by raising a final toast for the growth and further strengthening of the relations between the Soviet Armed Forces and the People's Revolutionary Armed Forces of Grenada.

In conclusion, it should be pointed out that the entire meeting was conducted in an atmosphere of warmth, friendliness, simplicity and unpretentiousness.

The meeting ended with warm embraces.

Bernard Bourne

[signature]

Minister-Counselor

Meeting with East German Premier
25 May 1983

The Prime Minister of East Germany (German Democratic Republic, or GDR), Willi Stoph, is quoted here as echoing Ogarkov's remark on the revolutionary situation in the Caribbean region: 'Cuba, Nicaragua and Grenada were the countries of greatest hope in the Caribbean region and it was their intention to seek to stabilise and support these revolutionary processes.' In his reply, the Grenadian Ambassador in

Moscow (W. Richard Jacobs, not named in the memorandum) disclosed that the NJM government held regular meetings with 'progressive parties in the region', with a view to 'improve the chances for progressive change in the other Caribbean islands'—in other words, to bring communism to these other islands.

EMBASSY OF GRENADA IN THE USSR

Dobryninskaya Ulitsa 7
Apartment 221
Moscow
USSR

Telephone
237–25–41
237–99–05

YEAR OF POLITICAL AND ACADEMIC EDUCATION

MEETING WITH PRIME MINISTER (CHAIRMAN OF THE COUNCIL OF MINISTERS) OF THE GDR, 20/5/83, 1:30 p.m.

The Prime Minister welcomed the Ambassador and congratulated him on his recent presentation of Credentials. He said that the formal conditions were now established for the development of close relations between Grenada and the GDR which after all were very new having started in June 1982 with the visit of the Prime Minister.

The Ambassador thanked the Prime Minister for his welcome, extended greetings from Prime Minister Maurice Bishop—who had found memories of his very warm reception in the GDR.

The Prime Minister responded that the GDR also had warm memories of Prime Minister Maurice Bishop's visit and he assured the Ambassador that the GDR will do everything necessary to fulfill all agreements reached between the GDR and Grenada and would, to the extent of its capacity, give further aid. He said that in the view of the GDR Cuba, Nicaragua and Grenada were the countries of greatest hope in the Caribbean region and it was their intention to seek to stabilize and support these revolutionary processes.

The Ambassador informed the Prime Minister that the GDR analysis of these countries was in line with the analysis of our Government and Party on these matters. Even so, we were working resolutely to improve the chances for progressive change in the other Caribbean islands. This required us to hold regular meetings with the progressive parties in the region. In the case of Grenada the internal counter-revolutionary activity was under control, but US imperialism was attempting to promote counter-revolution externally. Our people have demonstrated their determination to resist all imperialist intervention and by their hard work have demonstrated their determination to build the revolutionary process.

The Prime Minister said that the Government, people and Party of the GDR are impressed with the progress made by the Grenada revolution. He was informed about our further plans for co-operation in the field of radio and he was of the view that this was a particularly important undertaking. He hoped that it would be implemented quickly. The Prime Minister promised the full support of his office in the successful implementation of the duties of the Ambassador.

The meeting ended.

Grenada–Soviet Relations
11 July 1983

Grenada's alignment with Moscow is more clearly spelt out in this document than in any other in the collection. It is a Report, marked 'Confidential', from the Grenadian Ambassador to the USSR, W. Richard Jacobs, and was personally typed by him, for transmission to the NJM leaders, Maurice Bishop, Bernard Coard, Ewart Layne (a member of the NJM Politburo) and Unison Whiteman (a farmer's son who studied at the well-known black college, Howard University, in Washington, DC, and went on to be a co-founder of the New Jewel Movement, and Foreign Minister under Bishop. He was killed by the Coard faction).

Jacobs noted Cuba's championship of the NJM regime as a main reason for Soviet support. He records, however, that the Soviet Latin American expert Kasimirov had expressed dissatisfaction with the Grenadians for not having consulted the Soviets on their meeting with the US National Security Adviser, Judge William Clark, which he had first learned about from the press.

In an interesting passage the Ambassador declares: 'Our revolution has to be viewed as a world-wide process with its original roots in the Great October Revolution.' Grenada's importance in Soviet eyes was due to this fact and would grow in line with its sponsorship of 'revolutionary activity and progressive developments' in the Caribbean region. All relevant meetings in the region should be immediately reported to the Soviets. He named Surinam as the most likely candidate for special attention: 'If we can be an overwhelming influence on Surinam's international behaviour, then our importance in the Soviet scheme of things will be greatly enhanced.'

The opening lines of the Report are of semantic significance to students of international communism. 'Grenada,' wrote Jacobs, 'is regarded as being on the path of socialist orientation. There is general acceptance among Soviet authorities that we are at the national democratic, anti-imperialist stage of socialist orientation.' The term 'national democratic', or 'States of National Democracy', was launched at the end of 1960 in the World Communist Declaration which crowned a conference of eighty-one communist parties in Moscow. It was to be applied to various anti-colonial and 'anti-imperialist' regimes (such as those in Cuba, Egypt, Algeria, etc.) which were judged to be on the right lines—that is, heading for socialism and communism but not yet truly socialist.

Jacobs also mentioned that 'the Comrades responsible for Grenada in the International Section' had told him that they regarded the New Jewel Movement as a 'communist party'. He was, of course, referring to the International Department of the Central Committee of the Communist Party of the Soviet Union (CPSU), the effective successor to Lenin's Comintern, with a determining influence on Soviet foreign policy and on subversion, world-wide.

Key factors affecting the Soviet readiness to recognise the NJM as a communist party were listed. They included 'the policy on the communication media, the close links with the masses, the practice of popular democracy and the implementation of the policy of democratic centralism as a guiding principle and not a dogma'. Once more, we are in the realm of ideological semantics. The NJM was being praised for taking full control of the media, for having created State-controlled organisations, of trades unions, of youth and so forth, deemed to speak in the name of the 'people'; and for the system of binding acceptance of Politburo decisions by the rank-and-file of the party ('democratic centralism').

EMBASSY OF GRENADA IN THE USSR

Dobryninskaya Ulitsa 7   *Telephone*
Apartment 221   *237–25–41*
Moscow   *237–99–05*
USSR

Typed personally by W. Richard Jacobs.
Distribution as follows: Minister Unison Whiteman
                                        PM
                                        Deputy PM Coard
                                        PB Member Ewart Layne who is in
                                        the USSR

                                        11th July 1983

CONFIDENTIAL

GRENADA'S RELATIONS WITH THE USSR

Our relations with the USSR are influenced by a number of inter-connecting factors. Among the more important are:
1. Perceived ideological direction of the NJM Party and the PRG
2. The management of state affairs.
3. The development of state to state relations.
4. Grenada's role in the world (region).
5. Our relationship with other members of the socialist community.
6. Relationship between the NJM and CPSU.
7. Our activity in international organizations.

PERCEIVED IDEOLOGICAL DIRECTIONS—PRG

Grenada is regarded as being on the path of socialist orientation. There is a general acceptance among Soviet authorities that we are at the national democratic, anti-imperialist stage of socialist orientation. The USSR assigns a special place to these types of countries in its foreign policy. This is, of course, also the case with other socialist countries. In terms of their priorities, the countries of socialist orientation come right after the socialist community. Therefore, whatever the internal debate, it is important that we continue to maintain our public assessment of our stage of development as the national democratic, anti-imperialist stage of socialist orientation. After all the PM himself made that assessment when he was here in Moscow as well as during his visit to Berlin. This has recently been reinforced by the Foreign Minister during his visit to Vietnam, Kampuchia and Laos. So it seems to me absolutely necessary that we maintain this line. This is made all the more important by the very high priority that is placed on consistency of analysis here.

NJM

The Comrades responsible for Grenada in the International Section, have told me that they operate on the basis that the NJM is a "communist party". Given the relatively low level of these comrades (Nicholi etc.) one is not so sure about the authoritativeness of this statement though, I doubt that they would make a statement like that without the necessary authority. In any event, my clear impression is that we are being treated as a fraternal party—i.e. a M-L Party. My impression too, is that the CPSU delegation that visited in March formed a positive impression of the work of the NJM and have communicated that impression. The CPSU is in a position to know almost everything about the NJM—its size, programme, objectives, orientation etc. and they cannot fail to recognize and accept the authenticity of our credentials. The problem of protocol—the proper level at which our leaders should be met etc. remains. This could perhaps be explained on two levels: 1. They sometimes adopt an over-protective attitude towards us and argue that if we meet at too high a level the USA would use this as an issue to further squeeze Grenada. (This is one of the explanations floated as to why the PM did not meet with Andropov in April). 2. Although we are regarded as a fraternal party we are not in the "inner group" in members of the socialist community—their highest party officials are reserved for these levels of encounters. Their answer as to why Nicaragua is treated differently—and at a higher level—would presumably be that Nicaragua is already under direct US attack and it is necessary for them to openly show solidarity. They would like Grenada to avoid that direct attack. The core of the matter however, is that they regard Grenada as a small distant country and they are only prepared to make commitments to the extent of their capacity to fulfill, and if necessary, defend their commitment. (I recall on one occasion explaining the situation in St. Vincent to the Party comrades. Their response was that this is all very interesting but St. Vincent is so far away!!)

RECOMMENDATIONS

1. The Soviets have a correct perception of our ideological line both at the Government and Party levels. We should continue along these lines.

2. The problem of "protocol" has to be solved but it must be handled gently. At the diplomatic level, we could keep on insisting that counter-parts meet. To the extent that this is not achieved, the principals could mention it in passing—not a substantive point, just in passing. We must not fail to mention the matter to their Ambassador at social activities. Gestures are also important—cutting conversations short with junior people etc. Receprosity is also important. PB members should not be easily available to low-ranking Soviet officials on visits. As a rule, the PM in particular, and I would also say the Deputy PM should only entertain courtesy calls not exceeding 15 to 30 minutes.

THE MANAGEMENT OF STATE AFFAIRS

The Soviets have been burnt quite often in the past by giving support to Governments which have either squandered that support, or turned around and become agents of imperialism, or lost power. One is reminded of Egypt, Somolia, Ghana and Peru. They are therefore very careful, and for us sometimes maddingly slow, in making up their minds about who to support. They have decided to support us for two main reasons. 1. Cuba has strongly championed our cause. 2. They are genuinely impressed with our management of the economy and state affairs in general. They are impressed with our commitment to planning, the absence of corruption, the ethic of hard work among the leadership, the ability of the leadership to spread this ethic among the population, the willingness of sacrifice. They are also impressed with the policy on the communication media, the close links with the masses, the practice of popular democracy and the implementation of the policy of democratic centralism as a guiding principle and not a dogma. Also of importance is the stability of our leadership.

RECOMMENDATION

The Soviets are very impressed with our management of state power. We should continue along this line with a continuing emphasis on the "step by step" approach.

DEVELOPMENT OF STATE TO STATE RELATIONS

The principal item here is the implementation of the Agreements signed in July 1982. In the area of *Trade and Collaboration*—this is generally being implemented in accordance with the agreements. Some collaboration agreements however, have been delayed as a result of procrastination on our part. In particular, the sattelite dish agreement has not yet been signed by our side. As far as the Soviets are concerned, this is the centerpiece of our July agreements, the only negotiable items in it are how we house and transport the technicians, and how we pay them in local currency. The other items are fixed. The credit for this project cannot be utilized for any other project. We really need to get on with this matter. The same holds true for the Fifteen Teachers project. In any event, the reasons for not signing these agreements promptly, should be routinely communicated to the Embassy. We are not infrequently faced with the question as to what is the state of affairs on this or that project and we are placed in the very embarassing position of not being able to answer. Meanwhile, our Soviet colleagues who ask these questions often know the answer because their Embassy in Grenada has informed them. But even with these shortcomings, I would say that we are OK in this area of trade and collaboration.

State to state relations are also fundamentally influenced by the development of relations in other fields as well. We have a good record of collaboration at the military and trade union levels. These are positive factors in the development of our state to state relations. A lot more could be done at the NYO and Peace levels. It is important always to remember that plans for visits and interchanges should be made at least one year in advance. The NYO level is developing satisfactorily.

One of the most difficult areas is at the University and Technical education levels. As in all the above, the Soviets assess the level of state to state relations by, among other things, the extent to which we are willing to share our experiences with them, and learn from their experiences. When trade unionists, youth, women and pioneers come to study in the USSR, we are in effect signaling to them that we recognize that we can learn from their experiences and thereby sending the correct ideological message as well. The same holds true for our University and technical students. The presence of ten of our top planners has made a very favourable impact on the development of our state to state relations. But the same is not true in the area of the University and Technical education. To date we have been offered 80 (eighty) University or Technical scholarships—20 in 1981, 20 in 1982 and 40 in 1983. We have accepted eighteen (18) of which two of our students have given up the course. Of the remaining sixteen (16) at least eight (8) do not have the minimum requirements for entry to the level of education they expected to receive upon leaving Grenada. This, it seems to me, is requesting more than we know that we can absorb. It is much better to ask for five scholarships and fill four than to ask for 40 and send only four people. This gives the impression, false as it may be, that our students prefer not to study in the USSR. It introduces a certain question mark and works in a negative way on state to state relations. Of course, it need hardly be mentioned that the behaviour of our students can also have an effect on state to state relations, and we must therefore be careful to select highly motivated students.

The establishment of the Grenada-Soviet Friendship society has a positive effect on our relations. It is now critical that this organization *function*.

State to state relations are very seriously affected by the use that is made of the aid and assistance rendered to Grenada at the material and technical levels. In the case of technicians, it is important that proper provisions be made for their stay in Grenada and they be fully utilized for the entire time of their stay in Grenada. In general we have received very good feedback on this aspect and the technicians are full of praise for the enthusiasm and commitment of their Grenadian hosts.

In the case of the use of materials, the feedback has also been generally good. But there have evidently been some lapses, and we must always take care to ensure that we order the correct item with full information and specifications for everything asociated with its use. The case of the first set of tractors which arrived without the necessary attachments simply because the Soviets did not know what "attachments" we were talking about; the case of waterpumps going unused because of no hose; and the case of military vehicles without spare-parts in part because of poor specifications on our part—all contribute to a negative impression. There seems to have been some slip-up also in relation to the AN-2. The information needed for certification should certainly have been requested *before* the completion of the assembly of the plane. The Soviets have serious concerns about the operation and maintenance of the AN-26. We have assured them that we have a suit-able stand-by agreement with the Cubans on this one, but it is urgent that we select and dispatch as soon as possible ten (10) people—at least—to be trained for the operation and maintenance of this aircraft.

An important aspect of the development of state to state relations is the operation and functioning of the Embassy. All countries use the quality and quantity of personnel assigned as diplomatic staff to particular Embassies as an indication of the nature of a country's priorities in domestic and international affairs. The Soviet Union is no exception in this regard. Their own Embassy in Grenada is not only an indication of their resource base, but equally a reflection of the fact that they have considerable interest in the development of relations with Grenada.

I have on a previous occasion pointed out that for any Embassy to operate efficiently, the following officers are absolutely essential—Ambassador, Deputy (at the level of 1st Secretary or above) Secretary to the Ambassador, Accountant. This is emphasized even more in the case of the Embassy in Moscow by the fact that the Ambassador is accredited to nine other countries—GDR, Bulgaria, Checoslovakia, Hungary, Korea, Rumania, Mongolia, Poland, Yougoslavia and Afghanistan—ten in fact—and at least the first five plus the USSR are countries with which we have some serious relations. This means that the job requires a lot of travel. Both inside and outside the USSR, I would say that about 60% of the Ambassador's work is represen-tational. This responsibility requires two essential elements. 1. Infor-mation from Grenada. 2. Sophisticated analyses of the information available from each country. The first one is lacking but I am confident that a political decision can correct this situation. The second requires a person of high cultural level with some formal training and/or experience in international relations. Equally, we need someone with the appropriate training to undertake the task associated with the maintenance and development of our trading relations with the socialist community. Because of the structure of the diplomatic corps in the USSR both of these people need to be at the level of 1st. Secretary or above. We have a mountain of experience in the proper selection of these people. The fact is that a trained person can absorb and apply the experience to which he exposed in a creative way. An untrained person can be little more than a messenger, and length of service becomes a repetitive experience. It is important too, to recognize that particularly in the socialist community, training is highly valued and contributes to the development of the kind of prestige necessary to achieve our objectives.

All members of our leadership with whom I have raised this matter of staffing agree that we need additional staff at the Embassy in Moscow. This matter should be given the most urgent attention. Inadequate staff prevents this Embassy from developing state to state relations to the level necessary to preserve and advance our interests.

I mentioned earlier about the representational role of the Ambassador and the need for information for this task to be properly performed. I wish to draw on the example of the PM's recent mission to the USA. I was in the GDR at the time of the mission and I happened to hear on VOA a report of the PM's mission just before a meeting with the Foreign Ministry. The PM's mission turned out to be the main item on the agenda. I was able to handle the issue because as part of the information package on the March mobilization, the PS (Foreign Affairs) had sent an up-to-date package on our relations with the USA. When I returned to Moscow, the issue was raised by Kasimirov— Director of the First Latin American Department—who handles Grenada's affairs in the Foreign Ministry. Basically, he wanted to know what was the nature of the meeting with Clark. I told him that thus far the results are confidential. He said to me in the usual light vein of types of conversations that if he were friends with the American Ambassador he could get the information from him!! The basic point that he successfully got over to me is that in the circumstances of our relations with the USSR and their and our relations with the USA, it would have been courteous to inform them of the intention to visit. I agree with that. The contents of the discussion with Clark is another matter since, among other things, I am certain that the USA could break our code if they wanted to. Kasimirov told me that he first read of the visit in the newspapers and that he first heard that the PM had a meeting with Clark when the Canadian Ambassador, who was on a visit to his office, mentioned it to him. I feel sure that either his Ambassador in Grenada or USA would have informed him of this but the basic point that he is making is that he would have expected the information to come from me.

The other piece of information which is really crucial for our state to state relations deals with the IMF loan that I understand that we are negotiating or have signed. Now, when the PM raised the possibility of a US$6 million with Gromyko in April he made the point that we could get the money nowhere else. I have been monitoring the response here and the latest thing that they told me is that we may get a reply by mid July. I assume that the IMF loan has nothing to do with the airport project and therefore we are still going ahead with the US$6 million request which is strictly for the airport. But this is only an educated guess on my part. I have no hard information, and it would have been appropriate to let the Soviets know through our Embassy here that we were about to apply for this loan. Of course as I understand it, they have no problem with us going to the IMF. But the communication of this kind of information adds to a stable, reliable friendly state to state relations atmosphere. And equally important, it develops an expectation of recoprosity—they will give us information in the future.

RECOMMENDATIONS

1. We should make every effort to implement all collaboration and personnel-exchange agreements. In the case of personnel exchange, when it is not possible for the Grenada party to fulfill the agreement, the Embassy must be promptly informed. No individual should arrive in the USSR without previously informing the Embassy.

2. Both the Embassy and an appropriate Unit in the Ministry of Trade should monitor the implementation of trade agreements on a monthly basis and exchange this information. The Embassy and the Ministry of

Planning should do the same thing with other collaboration agreements. (I have in the past received such a monitoring report from the Macro-Planning Unit. But only on one occasion.)

3. We should as a matter of principle never request materials and opportunities that we are not in a position to utilize within a defined period.

4. A political decision should be immediately communicated to the International Department of the Party or the PS (Foreign Affairs) to keep the Embassy informed on all important issues.

5. Urgent steps be taken to recruit three new members of the diplomatic staff for the USSR Embassy with the appropriate qualifications.

GRENADA'S ROLE IN THE WORLD (REGION)

By itself, Grenada's distance from the USSR, and its small size, would mean that we would figure in a very minute way in the USSR's global relationships. Our revolution has to be viewed as a world-wide process with its original roots in the Great October Revolution. For Grenada to assume a position of increasingly greater importance, we have to be seen as influencing at least regional events. We have to establish ourselves as the authority on events in at least the English-speaking Caribbean, and be the sponsor of revolutionary activity and progressive developments in this region at least. At the same time, we have to develop and maintain normal state to state relations with our neighbours and concretely operationalize our good-neighbourlyness policy. The twice per year meetings with the progressive and revolutionary parties in the region is therefore critical to the development of closer relations with the USSR. In order to keep both the Embassy and the Soviets informed of the outcome of such meetings, perhaps a good model would be for a member of the CC to pay a visit to the USSR after each such meeting. The mission of such a person could without difficulty be mixed with other activities. We must ensure though that we become the principal point of access to the USSR for all these groups even to the point of having our Embassy serve as their representative while in USSR.

Equally important is our relationship with those neighbours who the Soviets regard as our potential adversaries. We have not been making a big deal of the Regional Defence Force but the Soviets never fail to mention that to their mind this is one of the most serious future dangers that we face. It is perhaps possible to use the CC on some kind of good-will mission to the other islands as a preliminary to the signing of some type of treaty of Friendship and Co-operation with them. It seems to me too, that we need to maintain a high diplomatic profile in these islands.

Of all the regional possibilities, the most likely candidate for special attention is Surinam. If we can be an overwhelming influence on Surinam's international behaviour, then our importance in the Soviet scheme of things will be greatly enhanced. To the extent that we can take credit for bringing any other country into the progressive fold, our prestige and influence would be greatly enhanced. Another candidate is Belize. I think that we need to do some more work in that country.

RECOMMENDATIONS

1. Establish a system of informing the Soviets of the outcome of the meetings between NJM and the progressive parties in the region.

2. Maintain these party to party meetings.

3. Examine the possibility of concluding formal treaties of Friendship and cooperation with our neighbours.

4. Explore ways and means of influencing the international behaviour (voting at UN etc.) of Surinam and Belize.

OUR RELATIONSHIP WITH OTHER MEMBERS OF THE SOCIALIST COMMUNITY

It is well to remember that there is a constant and very detailed consultation process that takes place between members of the socialist community. For example, on my recent mission to the GDR (June 1983) they made it very clear to me that they had been briefed on the PM's discussions with Gromyko, and this is to be expected. As a result, our performance in various aspects of our relations with members of the socialist community directly affects our relations with the USSR—not to mention the fact that it directly determines the relationship between Grenada and the country involved.

There have been some positive points that has promoted our image throughout the socialist community. Among the most recent are: 1. The excellent to very good performance of our students who went to the CPSU Party school—this has become generally known. 2. The excellent contribution made by comrade DeRiggs and the generally good impression made by the Grenada delegation at the Berlin Conference on Karl Marx—this is a constant cause of congratulations in various countries. (Incidentally, as a further indication of the communication problem, it is worth noting that I have not yet received a copy of this presentation which I am sure will serve as a good guide of policy.) 3. The fact that I have been presenting credentials and participating in the important occasions of the states involved. But there have also been negative factors. I think chief among them is the very slow process of implementing the agreements signed between Grenada and Bulgaria and GDR. This is very bad for our relations with the countries involved as well as for the USSR because they not only look at the process of implementation of our bi-lateral agreements with them, but also with the rest of the community. In particular, the GDR has floated the view with me that we appear to want to rewrite a solemn agreement agreed to by their President and our PM. (This refers prin-cipally to the method of paying for the bananas.) This, to them, is entirely inconceivable. My own view is that once the agreement is signed at that level, there is no going back and even if it is disadvan-tageous to us we just have to implement it. It is indecent to be seen as wanting to revise an agreement arrived by the two Heads of Govern-ment. I have no evidence that this view regarding our apparent desire to revise a solemn agreement has been communicated to other members of the community, but I would be very surprised if it has not. In any event, I have not formed the impression that there is any such generalized view within the community and it is of course in our interest to ensure that we retain the reputation as honest brokers who keep their word regardless. It is worth noting also that any effort to revise an agreement signed by the two Heads of Government *below* the level of Heads of Government will be next to impossible and could only serve to undermine the prestige and authority of the office of the Prime Minister.

As far as the relations with the other socialist countries are concerned, it is useful to have our people visit there as frequently as possible as well as to have state officials visit us as frequently as possible. I think that officials who travel to Eastern Europe should as a matter of policy include on their itinerary, at least one other socialist country in a planned and rotational way so that we get to touch as many bases as possible. If we are informed of such visits at least ten days in advance, we can get the host country, I am sure, to stand most of the costs. The benefits to us will be very great. As a rule, our officials have made a very positive impression on their hosts.

RECOMMENDATIONS

1. Continue high profile, well prepared participation in important events of the socialist community, eg Karl Marx Conference and World Peace Council.

2. Implement agreements between Grenada and other members of the socialist community promptly and faithfully.

3. Encourage officials to visit at least two countries in Eastern Europe during official missions to this part of the world.

PARTY TO PARTY RELATIONS

In the socialist community, it has emerged that there is a very close inter-relationship between party to party and state to state relations. Many of the things that the party was able to arrange in Cuba (eg airline tickets and special considerations of several kinds) are passed on to the state here. Further, as we discovered during the PM's mission and after, there is such an intimate linkage between the party and state at all levels, and notably at the highest levels that the distinctions that we have been inclined to make are not applicable in the socialist community.

One of the direct consequences of this is that the perception of party to party relations is fundamentally influenced by the nature of state to state relations and it is important to constantly keep this in mind.

Of course the implementation of the party to party agreements is paramount. By and large, we have implemented these agreements faithfully. Our first batch of party school students, although they were some two years late, have made a very good impression. Our implementation of the rest and recreation agreements have been good for our relationship. But there are a number of negative points. I think the most telling is the fact that Comrade Strachan undertook during his mission here in December to send a team of party mobilizers to the USSR for a couple of weeks to experience the Soviet experience. As is known, these people were not sent. This did some damage which could have been minimized if we had received some instructions to explain to the CPSU comrades that this undertaking was not possible at the moment. As it is, they cancelled it when the time ran out. Another example, has to do with the Public address system. We said that we needed it urgently for March 13th, 1983. They rushed it down by air to Cuba at the end of January, as promised, and the P.A. system stayed in Cuba for a very long time. I am not even sure if it has arrived as yet. They have brought this matter to our attention on a number of occasions, we have sent messages to Cuba and Grenada to try and co-ordinate our excuses but we have received no response.

We have to insist too that they stick to their agreements, for example, they agreed with Comrade Strachan to send down to Grenada "a high level delegation"—in March 1983—you know of course, the very low level that was sent. They also agreed to send two people for rest and recreation in 1983, and we must make sure their undertakings to supply books, magazines, newspapers, films and projection equipment for the political education programme. We have to stick them to their word. I can raise it here at the diplomatic level but it will be twice as effective when it is repeated at the party political level.

The problem of what might be called counterpart protocol remains. That is, we have never been able to meet with our strict counterparts at the party level when we have our leaders here. On 27th June, I had a very frank and friendly discussion with Boyko Demitrov—the former Bulgarian Ambassador to Grenada who is now Director of International Relations in the Party. He told me that even Bulgaria sometimes faces this problem and that Grenada has to face the reality that it is a question of size, distance and priorities. I think that he is correct. But we then have to deal with these realities. In order to elevate our priority in the socialist scheme of things, the recommendations contained in the section dealing with our role in the world (region) becomes all the more relevant. In addition, we have to raise and discuss with the highest authorities, *global* and regional issues rather than parochial or national issues. In other words, our legitimate beginning operations have to be cast in the larger world context. We have in fact done this in the past quite successfully, linking our national requests to a global analysis. What we need to do now, it seems to me, is to become the spokesman for a broader constituency—perhaps the countries of socialist orientation. It is in this context that I have prepared the attached paper dealing with a task of last resort sponsored by the socialist community for countries for socialist orientation. This will give us an opportunity to discuss the highest issues of policy both with the countries of socialist orientation and with the socialist community, lift our profile, and tighten our priority. Here we can clearly see the close link between party to party and state to state relations.

All that is said about the CPSU holds true for the other parties as well. We have a very sympathetic hearing in Bulgaria with Boyko Demitrov and we should perhaps draw ever closer to the Bulgarian Party.

In the GDR, we also have made a good impression and there is great sympathy there for the NJM. Four comrades will be coming for rest and recreation in 1983.

I doubt that we will encounter the protocol problems that we have found in the CPSU. But we must at all cost continue to regard relations with the CPSU at the highest priority.

RECOMMENDATIONS

1. Strictly implement all agreements and initiatives on implementation on the other sides as well.
2. Send prompt explanations when it is not possible to implement an agreement.
3. Seek to become spokesman for the countries of socialist orientation.
4. Develop even stronger relations with the Bulgarian and GDR parties by sending delegations etc.

INTERNATIONAL ACTIVITY

From the point of view of our relations with the USSR, our international activity is important from the following perspectives:

1. The consistency of our political line.
2. The influence of Grenada in the international community.
3. The degree of support offered to the positions taken by the USSR.

Our performance is assessed at the following levels:

1. The United Nations and its agencies—UNESCO, UNCTAD etc.
2. Organization of American States
3. Non-aligned Movement
4. Missions in various countries (Embassies).

It is very difficult for me to assess their view of our performance in the UN, its agencies and the OAS because, we receive only the minimum of information on our voting and performance etc. But during the period of the threats etc., in March 1983, they advised us to play a more active role in the UN especially at the Security Council and spoke approvingly of Nicaragua's performance at the Security Council. But I suspect that we need a bigger staff at the UN to do the kind of job that would impress internationally. The same probably holds true for the OAS. They have however, praised our role in the Zone of Peace resolution and activity.

At the non-aligned movement, they have a high valuation of our role. You will recall that before the New Delhi Conference they gave me a detailed briefing on their positions and when Comrade Whiteman visited afterwards they expressed admiration for our performance. I think however, that we must insist that we form the inner circle of the advisers to Mrs. Gandhi in line with our leading role in New Delhi especially in regard to the New International Economic Order and the Small States Conference. We have an excellent case—especially since Guyana did not participate when they were invited to in May 1983 in New Delhi. The Guyana Ambassador here tells me that the Foreign

Minister decided that the Heads of Mission meeting then taking place in Guyana was more important.

As far as our Embassies are concerned, the most important thing is that they carry the same line on all matters—economic and political, internal and external. To do this successfully, we need to have a common fund of information. Obviously, each mission would have its area of speciality and would have more information on that area than any other Embassy. But a regular series of directives, instructions and information from the Party or the Foreign Ministry would ensure that a common line is maintained throughout.

As far as the role of the mission in the USSR is concerned, the reality of size came to me very early in the game. It therefore became necessary to establish ones influence in the corps by making strategic associations and alliances. Latin America—our natural constituency—lacks cohesiveness and leadership. The Dean of the Latin American group—Venezuela is lazy and uninterested in leadership. The Cuban Ambassador is not very out-going. So I have had to maintain individual relationships especially with Cuba, Nicaragua and Mexico. Ecuador is also a good man. The African group is much more cohesive and influential in Moscow. They have also been very welcoming. My informal inclusion in the group has raised Grenada's profile and influence in the corps as a whole.

The socialist countries to which I am accredited are a [illeg.] area of interest. Of these, Bulgaria is the Dean and has little time for socio-political interaction. Checoslovakia, GDR and Rumania have been particularly warm. We have it as a high priority to establish and maintain the closest personal and official relations with these countries. And although the Korean Ambassador for example, is regarded as a recluse, I have had him over to dinner and he has reciprocated, as is the case with many of the others.

On the whole, I have formed the view that the USSR is satisfied with the degree of support that they receive from Grenada. Indeed, I would say that they have every reason to be satisfied especially if our vote on Afganistan for example, is recognized as one of two Latin American votes (the other being Cuba) in their favour. Considering the risks that we have taken on this and other matters, it might be fair to say that their support for us is actually below our support for them. We must therefore work to establish a balance of interests. This might best be done by gentle reminders at critical stages by members of our leadership. We might also seek to develop our links with what has been called the "middle" countries like Yugoslavia and Greece for example and strengthen our links with "off centre" countries like Korea, Rumania and Hungary. But these calculations have to be done very carefully and in a very sophisticated way. We have to think them out very carefully.

RECOMMENDATIONS

1. Continue our international support for the Soviet line.

2. Strengthen our political efforts in the UN and OAS and their agencies.

3. Seek a more critical role in the non-aligned movement.

4. Examine the desirability, ways and means of developing closer relations with the "middle" and "off centre" countries.

5. Provide all missions with a regular common fund of knowledge so that there can be a guarantee that a common line is being pursued on all matters.

Student Training in Moscow. Report 1
23 May 1983

This document and the next refer to training courses for Grenadian students at 'the CPSU party school', described in the second of the documents as the 'International Leninist School'. The reference is presumably to the CPSU's Lenin Institute, also known by a variety of other names, including the Lenin School, the Institute of Social Sciences, the Institute of Social Studies and the International School of Marxism–Leninism. All these names are interchangeable and refer to a party teaching (i.e. indoctrination) academy under the direct control of the Soviet Communist Party's Central Committee. The students come from Moscow-line communist parties in Europe, the Americas, the Arab world, Asia and Africa. Some of them are selected for terrorist and guerrilla training in courses lasting six months.

The first Report was written by Grenada's Ambassador, W. Richard Jacobs, and gives a detailed account of the training received by the Grenadian students.

EMBASSY OF GRENADA IN THE USSR

Dobryninskaya Ulitsa 7	Telephone
Apartment 221	237–25–41
Moscow	237–99–05
USSR	

Course name: WCM—World Communist Movement
SPP—Social Psychology and Propaganda
—Historic Experience of the CPSU

Name of Students

School name	*Real name*
Femr Achebe	Derrick James
David Gill	Sam Braithwaite
Justin Lorainey	Fabian Outram
Bill Jordan	Anselm DeBourg
Francis Che	Glen Noel
Bernadine Peters	Rita Joseph
David Allen	Ian Lambert
Dave Gordon	Andre McQueen
John Franklyn	Ronnie Spooner
—	William St. Louis
—	Gordon Raeburn
—	Roy Cooper
—	Patrick Superville
—	Fred Burris

EMBASSY OF GRENADA IN THE USSR

Dobryninskaya Ulitsa 7	Telephone
Apartment 221	237–25–41
Moscow	237–99–05
USSR	

Report of meeting with Acting Rector of the CPSU party school Gaiduz Oleg P. 23rd, May 1983

This meeting between the Acting Rector and the Ambassador was arranged at the request of the Ambassador to receive a confidential assessment of the performance of our students during the six-month course just completed.

The Acting Rector informed the Ambassador that normally, it is necessary to apply to the International Department of the CPSU in order to receive an official report of the performance of the students. However, in this case, since this was the first batch of Grenadian students he would be prepared to make available to the Party (NJM) the confidential assessments of their teachers as well as to communicate to the Ambassador in a confidential manner, the general opinion of the teachers regarding the overall performance of our students. The Ambassador thanked the Acting Director for his cooperation in that matter and pointed out that he will also request an official report from the CPSU.

The Acting Director reported that since this was the first group of Grenadians to attend the school, it was the policy of the administrators and teachers to pay very close and careful attention to the performance and behaviour of the students. After a collective assessment of the students, he could inform the Ambassador that he was expressing the unanimous opinion of the teachers and administrators of the school.

The students fully covered the syllabus of the six month course. It was the view of the school however, that the students would have benefited more from a one year course.

As a whole the students were well disciplined and oriented towards collective work. Minor evidences of indiscipline were never repeated once they had been identified and explained.

The internal relations of the group were generally good. Friction was kept to a minimum, problems were resolved in time, and due to the excellent leadership of Rita Joseph, the collective maintained a very marked cohesion throughout the course. It is worthy of note that comrade Joseph was greatly helped in the exercise of her responsibility and authority by the following Comrades: Gordon Raeburn, Ronnie Spooner, Ian Lambert and Fabian Outram.

Comradely relations between members of the group steadily improved over the period of six months.

Attendance at classes was excellent, but punctuality was occasionally weak.

All comrades displayed a conscientious attitude towards their work.

With the sole exception of Fred Burris, our students actively participated in classroom discussions. They always adopted a very serious attitude towards the work, asked relevant questions and all except Burris have been assessed as having achieved good to excellent knowledge. Burris was satisfactory.

All the students made consistent efforts to link up the theoretical points with the tasks to which they have been assigned by the NJM. This was particularly true of Ian Lambert, Rita Joseph and Roy Cooper.

There was a marked difference in cultural levels of the students as well as in levels of health. Both Fred Burris and Andre McQueen (David Gordon) were ill for long periods. A Report on McQueen's illness is enclosed.

The group took several good initiatives, and undertook the responsibilities associated with these initiatives. Three examples: Celebration of the 10th. Anniversary of the NJM, 4th. Anniversary of the Revolution, Round table solidarity Conference of the Amaricas.

As part of their practical work, the group had a permanent link with the CPSU Party committee of the October factory. They went to the factory on several occasions, participated in voluntary work on two occasions and had a lecture on the cost accounting procedures of the factory. The management of the factory was pleased with the students' performance and the students were satisfied with their experience.

The two most outstanding students were: Rita Joseph and Ian Lambert. The weakest student was Fred Burris. The teachers considered that Burris would be well placed in an area of work requiring inter-personal relations with non-intellectual workers. He can carry out instructions and is very tenacious in his determination to implement agreed procedure, but he is neither an intellectual nor initiator.

The Acting Rector said that the performance of our students demonstrate a real thirst for knowledge and he recommended that the NJM think very seriously about the establishment of a Party School as a top priority. He pointed out that there were very positive achievements as a result of the establishment of the Party School in Yemen, Afganistan, Angola, Mozambique and very soon Ethiopia. In this context he suggested that the NJM might think of sending students who could qualify as teachers in the future Party School.

In closing the Acting Director said that he would like to emphasize that the teachers and Administrators had come to develop great respect for the abilities of Rita Joseph as a leader. In the beginning they were a bit apprehensive about her ability to manage thirteen men and she was a bit shakey in the beginning, but as time went on, it emerged that it was a wise decision.

[signature]

W. Richard Jacobs

Student Training in Moscow. Report 2
8 October 1983

This is a 'student's-eye' Report on the course offered at the Lenin Institute (see previous document). Obviously the course provided a thorough grounding in Marxism–Leninism, in party organisation and in propaganda activities and techniques. The NJM student notes the presence of colleagues from England and Germany (whether East or West was not specified), and from Nicaragua, Angola, Mozambique, Ethiopia, South Africa, Syria, Colombia, Denmark and Jamaica—a fairly representative 'mix' for the Lenin Institute.

The course began with a historical survey, starting with the forma-tion of the RSDLP (the Russian Social-Democratic Labour Party, which after various name-changes, became the Soviet Communist Party). The list of 'non-academic activities' ends with plans for the students to take part in the Soviet subbotnik, *a reference to a work-day (usually a Saturday,* subbota *in Russian) donated by workers to the State.*

8 October 1983
Moscow

Cde. Strachan,

Attached is the first report from the group for our first month's activity. Other things have happened since then but I will include them in the next report which I hope to send down with whoever comes to represent us at the November 7 activity.

Everything is basically alright—the course is going fine, but plenty work—writing, reading reporting, etc.

Since writing the report, Cde. [illeg.] has left for Moscow Central [illeg.].

We are anxious for a response to the report and further directives.

Greetings to everyone!

[illeg.]
[signature]
Hazel-Ann

REPORT TO N.J.M. ORGANISING COMMITTEE
FROM PARTY CELL AT CPSU INTERNATIONAL
1st–30TH SEPTEMBER, 1983

1. Introduction
2. Course Outline
3. Internal Structure
4. Cell Assessment
   Non-Academic Activities
6. Moscow Party Branch
7. Needs
8. Issues for Party's Attention & Decisions
9. Conclusions

I. INTRODUCTION

1.1 The Comrades comprising the party cell [illeg.] International Leninist School, as [illeg.] are—[illeg.] Neckles, Albert Alexander [illeg.] Bernadette Smith, [illeg.] Hazel Ann [illeg.]
1.2 We left Grenada 27th August for [illeg.] Havana. Flight problems resulted in our [illeg.] days in Cuba and arriving in Moscow [illeg.]
1.3 This report covers the period 1st [illeg.] They will continue during the acade [illeg.] monthly basis.

2 COURSE OUTLINE

2.1 Our classes started on September 6th with the Russian language which lasted for three (3) weeks amounting to fifty (50) hours. We completed this course by performing an Auction Sale in Russian for the school audience of mainly new students—Friday 30th.
2.2 The school week is from Monday to Saturday, with General Lectures on Monday and specific topics on the other days—up to Saturday.

2.3 Our present course is comprised by the following topics:
   i) Historical Experience of the CPSU
   ii) Internal Relations
   iii) Political Economy

iv) Philosophy

v) Theory & Tactics of the World Revolutionary Movement

The following gives an idea as to the subject matter we have completed or are presently doing under each topic:

NO. TOPIC	SUBJECT MATTER/SUB-TOPIC
1. Historical Experience - CPSU This topics ends on the 3rd week in March and our "Final Talks" is one week later.	— Formation of RSDLP — The Leninist Stage in the development of Marxism — Historic Destinies of Marx's Teachings — Ideological and Theoretical Foundation of the Leninist Party — Features of the Party of a New Type — Sections of "What Is To Be Done?"
2. International Relations This is short—Only 48 hours ending 1st week in December. No "Final Talks."	— Structure & General Features of International Relations — What is International Relations? — Peaceful Co-Existence concept — Proletarian internationalism — The three (3) sub-sections that exist in International Relations — Problems of War & Peace — Disarmament: USA-USSR Negotiations — War, Nuclear Weapons
3. Political Economy This ends 2nd week in April; "Final Talks" one week later.	— Economic Map of USSR — Capitalist Mode of Production & Stages of its development — Capitalism's Place In The History of Society — History of Society

4. Philosophy—Finishes 4th   — Emergence of Philosophy
    week in May; "Final Talks" —Development of Philosophical
    in 1st week of June.   Thinking in Ancient Greece
                                     — What is Philosophy?

5. Theory & Tactics of the   — Lenin's definition of Strategy
    World Revolutionary Move-   & Tactics
    ment. Finishes 2nd week of — Sections of the Communist
    May; "Final Talks" 3rd week   Manifesto: chapters 1 & 2
    of May.   — The First, Second & Third
                                     Internationals
                                   — The World Revolutionary Pro-
                                     cess In The Contemporary Epoch

2.2 Apart from these five topics, another three will be added upon completion of the initial five. The following explains:

NO.	TOPIC	STARTING DATE	COMPLETION DATE
1.	Party Organisation	4th week of December	3rd week of June
2.	Theory of Management of National Economy	4th week of April	3rd week of June
3.	Social Psychology & Propaganda	2nd week of December	2nd week in June

2.3 We are expected to participate in a theoretical conference from 3rd February–27th March on the topic—"A Revolutionary Party Is The Vanguard of Our Time." If possible, we will appreciate the Party's assistance in this regard—ideas for approach, content, creative application to our situation, etc.

2.4 Besides the theoretical party the school's plan is for us to participate in practicals. There will be two such activities.

3. CELL STRUCTURE

3.1   Monitors   :Merril
  ii) Hostel   :Deborah
  iii) Canteen   :Neckles(?!)

iv) Sports   :Albert
v) Culture   :Bernadette
vi) Group   Leaders   :Hazel-Ann

3.2 Our cell meetings are held forthnightly to discuss:
   i) Reports
   ii) Criticism & Self-criticism
   iii) Any Other Matters
   For the period, we have had two such meetings—5 and 19 September, each for a duration of about 90 minutes.
3.3 We have developed a system for checking individuals' level of preparation for classes by organising a study chart for comrades to mark their level using a scoring system of 0–5. However, we have to improve on the level of supervision of this to ensure that this works and achieves its objective.
3.4 Additionally, the cell meets four nights weekly for the purpose of collective study which entails revision of the subjects covered for the previous days and preparation for the next days class. It takes place on Monday, Wednesday and Friday from 9:00 p.m. - 11:00 p.m. and Sundays from 10:a.m. - 12:00 noon. But the Sunday time may vary depending on whether school activities are organised for that day.

4. CELL ASSESSMENT

4.1 The cell is close and very united. We have not had any internal problems as yet.
4.2 Cde. Neckles up to now has not been able to start his classes as yet because of ill health. The doctor's report is that he has high pertension and is sick with his heart. He has been kept in the isolation unit at the school, but is due to leave for the Central Moscow Hospital for medical treatment. No indication as to how long he will remain there has been given as yet.

   This is an area of concern for the group and one the Party will have to consider because the doctors have said that he must not study hard, but the work here requires hard study and already he has lost one month. The relevant decision will have to be taken by the Party.
4.3 Deborah Roberts was hospitalised for two weeks because of additional problems. She has now returned and is 'picking up' what she has missed in the period.

5. NON-ACADEMIC ACTIVITIES

5.1 We have had thorough medical examinations by—general physician, eye, bone, skin and ENT specialists, neurologist and dentist. We are [illeg.] to X-ray and heart examinations during the coming month.

5.2 The cell has been brought on two excursions organised by the school:
   i) Sunday, 11 September—Lenin's house in Gorky where he lived from 1918–1923.
   ii) Sunday, 18 September—Tour of Moscow: Red Square, Kremlin, etc.

5.3 We attended activities hosted by the English and German collectives to celebrate their respective parties' anniversaries.

5.4 Our cell has developed contacts with our colleagues in the Nicaraguan, Angolan, Mozambique, Ethiopian, South African, Syrian, Colombian and Denmark collectives. In particular, we have developed close contacts with the Jamaican collective, and also have contacts with other groups.
   Our active participation in sports has not started as yet. The same goes for culture.

5.6 On October 18 we will take part in the Soviet subbotnik—Soviet Voluntary [illeg.] work.

6. MOSCOW PARTY BRANCH

6.1 So far, we have attended one meeting and study session of the branch. All comrades have paid their September Party dues.

7. NEEDS

7.1 We need the following items for activities we will be having:
   — Party, Revolution, National Flags (all sizes)
   — Posters
   — Party Emblem
   — View cards
   — Large pictures or posters of leadership
   — buttons or tokens
   — Party Literature—Jewel, Posters, etc. . . .
   — Important taped speeches of the leadership

— Updated list of achievements
— local craft and other items—. . .

7.2Analysis of the present political situation

7.3Regular newspapers and other literature

8. ISSUES FOR PARTY'S ATTENTION & DECISIONS

8.1Resource material and ideas for our participation in the theoretical conference (Earliest)

8.2Issue of Cde. Neckle's illness [illeg.]

8.3We are all anxious as to whether arrangements made for salary payments are working properly.

8.4...

8.5A deputy leader of the group needs to be designated.

8.6We would appreciate a critical response to this report.

9. CONCLUSION

9.1The Party cell has been informed of the recent analysis, decisions and thinkings of the Central Committee.

9.2We first of all, congratulates the C.C. on having reached this conclusion and for what it signifies. We believe that it is one of the most (if not the most) positive developments in the Party's history because it really shows the Marxist-Leninist character or tendency of our Party and is a concrete manifestation of our proclaimed adherence to the Marxist-Leninist principle of constructive criticism and self-criticism from the highest to the lowest bodies within the organisation.

9.3For us, what we can do towards the solution of the crisis is of paramount importance for us to know. In the meantime, we have discussed the issue and have decided that under the present conditions, we pledge to take a more serious and Leninist approach to our ideological training.

9.4Our other specific questions, comments and suggestions have been done through the Party Branch.

9.5We take this opportunity to express our deep concern about the situation as analysed by the cc; our confidence in the Party's leadership and our collective ability to avert the situation through hard, organised systematic, self-critical, Leninist-type work. The CPSU International Leninist NJM Party Cell repledges our commitment to the Party; to building a strong Party on Marxist-Leninist principles and to the defense and building of the Revolution along the lines that would bring us to achieving Socialism.

Long Live our Party!

Hazel-Ann
Moscow
[illeg.]

5. THE NEW JEWEL MOVEMENT
AND THE CHURCHES

From the first, in line with the general rule of Marxist–Leninist regimes, the NJM government assumed an attitude of systematic hostility towards the Churches on Grenada.

Catholic Church Publications Report
11 February 1980

Although unsigned, this Report carries marginal notes in Maurice Bishop's handwriting. It refers in hostile terms to dissident Catholic Church publications distributed over the island.

TOP SECRET

REPORT   18.30 hrs.   FEBRUARY 11, 1980

A series of publications are being put out by the Catholic Church. Most of those published so far are aimed at showing that Communism is atheistic and should be feared and that our party is Communist. The articles aim at creating fear in the minds of the religious.

So far five have been published in the series—the first three being the small leaflets of track size. No.4 was Civic Freedoms, No.5 some notes on Marx-Leninism. The sixth publication is in the making but no definite date has been given as to when it will be out.

[Who types?]　　The typing of the 5th publication was done by an Irish teachers at St. John's Christian Secondary School.

[*Which priests + any others?*]　　Father Bernard Kadlec of Czechoslovakia is one of the writers. Father Austin is another. (I don't know which).

Publication is done by McKie's Printery, and Torchlight Printery. A track size publication Brown writing is now being printed in St. Lucia.

[*Where printed?*]

Further information could not be had: the Priest was in a haste to leave for St. George's.

However, the Priest said that whenever he publishes any of these things he always send one to the Prime Minister.

[X]　　He seems to have a lunch that the PRG will clamp down on these publications. I told him to ensure me a copy of each of his publications when he replied yet with a statement to this effect.

Father Bernard was the writer of Civic Freedoms, but I have not found out who is the author of the 5th publication.

The Priest is also afraid of these leaving the hands of the PRA soldiers for fear they may lose their jobs.

[*Source*]

And so fear to give it to soldiers.

Cuban Report on Churches
14 October 1982

This Report was prepared by the Americas Department of the Cuban Communist Party (PCC) and is undoubtedly one of the most important of the Grenada documents in that it reveals the extent of Cuban intervention in Grenadian affairs. Although it provides no direct evidence of Soviet intervention, it is clearly consistent with a desire on Cuba's part to ensure that the NJM's attitude towards the Catholic Church, in particular, is in line with Soviet policy.

In reality, the Catholic Church remained largely inactive during the period of NJM rule. The only point of dissension noted in this Report is indeed over the timetable for elections. True, the Church had wished to act as a mediator for political prisoners in Grenadian gaols, but in so doing it was merely acting in line with long-established tradition and not specifically in a spirit of hostility towards the NJM.

A close reading of the Report shows that Cuba was concerned not about any anti-regime words or deeds by the Church but about any potential *trouble along such lines. In so doing it appears to have tried to anticipate the kind of problem, on a smaller scale, which the Soviets have encountered with the Church in Poland.*

The measures recommended by the Cubans, especially the proposed 'Register of Associations', were clearly on totalitarian lines. In this context, the call for a special role for 'clergymen and members of the laity from Nicaragua and other Latin American circles linked to the theology of liberation' is particularly significant, as is the call for 'a church committed to the revolutionary positions'.

RESTRICTED

REPORT OF THE DELEGATION SENT TO GRENADA BY THE AMERICA DEPARTMENT WITH THE AIM OF START-ING THE GATHERING OF SOURCES FOR THE CHARACTERIZATION OF THE RELIGIOUS SITUATION IN THE COUNTRY, AND THE CONTACTS FOR FURTHER

COOPERATION BETWEEN THE PCC AND THE NJM RE-
GARDING THE QUESTION.

DELEGATION: Cde. Aurelio Alonso Tejada
DATE: August 13—24, 1982
This report was handed in on October 14, 1982,
    "YEAR 24 OF THE REVOLUTION"

INTRODUCTORY NOTE

This report is the result of an initial ten days stay which, as it coincided
with holidays, could not be used to the greatest advantage.

Two more difficulties must be taken into account: firstly, the total lack
of informative or unofficial documentation by the NJM comrades,
which resulted in the need to find sources through our visit to the public
library, the national museum, and religious bookstores; secondly, the
absence of Judy Williams, the most important person among the
Christian lay people that actively cooperate with the NJM who, in
addition to her personal testimonies, should have arranged our contacts
with othe rpositive elements within the laity. This situation caused our
interviews to be limited to representative sof the ecclesiastical
institutions.

In spite of these difficulties, it can be considered that the work showed
useful results so that the thought-out objectives were satisfactorily
reached.

We received a decisive support by the revolutionary leadership through
Cde. Selwyn Strachan, member of the Political Bureau of the NJM and
Minister of National Mobilization, whom we met on three occasions.
During the first interview, Cde. Strachan summarized the recent
aggressive positions adopted by the Church against the revolutionary
leadership and we, on our part, explained the concrete aims we had set
for the visit.

CONCLUSIONS

The religious situation in Grenada shows a series of characteristics
which can be summarized as follows:

1) Since the revolutionary triumph in 1979, the diocese showed signs of reservation and started to insist on the holding of elections. During the three years of revolutionary government, the Catholic hierarchy has added to its electoral claim a position of mediation in favor of the 1979 pro-Gairy prisoners and of advocate of the "freedom of the press" in the face of governmental measures to stop counterrevolutionary propaganda. The emphasis of the Church is in harmony with the campaigns carried out by the reactionary governments in the Caribbean against Grenada's PRG and now has an institutional argument formalized in the pastoral of the Caribbean Catholic bishops in February this year. This pastoral marks a new reference, which goes backward in comparison with that of 1975, and starting from it, political sectors in the area have promoted the summons to the Church for a confrontation of forces with the PRG of Grenada.

2) For the Grenadian Church (particularly the Catholic one) the moment can be described as one of definitions. It cannot be said yet (in our opinion) that the hierarchy has decided on an open confrontation. Although the pressure from the reactionary forces in the region within and outside the Church is aimed at confrontation, the position of the diocese seems to lean towards a combination of the pastoral attacks with repeated reference to the disposition to dialogue and the insistence upon the fact that their position towards the PRG is not uncompromising.

3) There are reasons to think that there is a potential contradiction between the foreign clergy (mainly the British and the Irish) and the West Indian minority. That majority, whom the vicar of the cathedral himself think is alien and unadaptable to the local realities, is at first sight the most active counterpart of the oppositionist dynamics brought about by the February pastoral and by the provocations of reactionary forces in the region.

4) There are no signs of systematic progressive projections within the Grenadian clergy. It seems that within the institution there is not a trend in the theological and social line sympathetic to the revolutionary project, and there are no indications of a community organization of this kind at the grass roots. However, some believers belonging to Catholic organizations, who gather around the Pope Paul Camp (with whom we could not get in touch during this visit) and who actively

collaborate with the NJM, can constitute a ferment in this direction.

5) The strong point of the Grenadian churches (both the Catholic and traditional Prostestant ones) regarding their social influence is the educational sector. The religious schools are, at a very high percent, in charge of elementary and secondary education because throughout the colonial period the State traditionally neglected this section. The PRG does not have a public educational system. In our opinion, the teaching centers are the stronghold of the ecclesiastical institutions and the possibility of a reform that should bring about their exclusion is their main concern.

6) The incorporation of the Catholic churches of the Caribbean to the Conference of CAribbean Churches (CCC), which also includes over 20 Protestant churches since its creation in 1973, besides being an exceptional characteristic of ecumenism, establishes an associational link among the Christian institutions that admots a game of influences in their projection: the Grenada Catholic diocese is a member of the Conference of Churches of Grenada (CCG) and with its positions it can influence on the Protestant churches, and the other way around; at the same time, the fact that the Catholic Church belongs to the CCC means a similar game of influences at the regional level. In this interaction, the most positive positions of the CCC act as a restraining factor to the behaviour of the Catholic Church at the local (and regional) level. However, the CCC is not a homogeneous body and the possibility of a resersal of its positions should no be under-estimated, which would be in harmony with the tone of the criticisms to the PRG by the Grenadian churches.

7) The estimated believing population is over 80 percent, made up mainly by Catholics (59 percent), Protestant from the historical churches (Anglicans, Presbyterians and Methodists), and a number of sects among which the Rastafarians seem to be widely disseminated. The level of participation observed in the Sunday service is high. There does not seem to exist a significant difference in the degree of religiosity among Protestants and Catholics. The Charismatic Catholic movement has expanded and it is thought to reach no less than a quarter of Catholics. The African roots and their possible syncretic expressions should be studied.

8) The Catholic Church is organized in a diocese with 20 parish churches. It has one Bishop and 22 priests, with a rate of one priest for every 2,950 Catholics (baptized). Sixteen of the priests are religious and 6 are diocesan; 16 are English, Irish, and American; 4 are from other West Indian countries and 2 from Grenada; 15 are white and 7 are mestizo or black. Thus, because of their origin and race this is a clergy with characteristics that alienate them from the problems of the island.

9) The diocese is suffragan to the archdiocese of Castries (St. Lucia) and belongs to the Episcopal Conference of the West Indies, whose main seats are Jamaica and Trinidad-Tobago. Thus the ecclesiastical organization takes on a supranational character and the projection of the Grenadian Church is linked to the strategy carried out by the West Indian body.

. . . .

RECOMMENDATIONS

1. We underline the importance of the fact that a comrade responsible for the attention to the religious problems be appointed by the New Jewel Movement: This activity would basically include the information work at the beginning and regular contacts with collaborators from Christian organizations. If it is thought to be relevant, this can also include contacts with the clergy. We repeat the recommendation that the person to be appointed should spend 15—20 days in Cuba so as to be able to know our experiences, be trained in the tasks of systematic information on the subject, and exchange ideas on the most con-troversial aspects of the work. Comrade Strachan expressed his agreement on this proposal.

2. It would be advisable to study the possibility of formally creating a Register of Associations (or a similar mechanism) attached to the corresponding governmental body. Such a body could be legally established on the basis of the public need to make an inventory of the existing associations in the country and their activities (this would not only include the religious institutions, but the Chamber of Commerce, associations of professionals, clubs such as the Rotarians, the Lions, etc.). This would enable the counting of members, posts, premises, etc.,

the knowledge on special and regular activities, the means of financing of activities, etc. Both the terms of the resolution or law and the concrete contents of the register and modus operandi would be defined according to the specific conditions. This proposal is based on the need to regularize the access by the PRG to systematic factual information on the religious institutions and their activities. Our recommendation does not dismiss the fact that the responsibility regarding the register could be closely linked to the above-mentioned proposal.

3. To promote contacts among clergymen and members of the laity from Nicaragua and other Latin American circles linked to the theology of liberation and, in general, to the idea of a church committed to the revolutionary positions, and the Christians sectors in Grenada through the Pope Paul Camp and maybe through talks with religious clergymen from a same order, particularly the Dominicans. These contacts should positively influence the Christian sectors of Grenada.

. . . .

ANNEX 2
SUMMARIES OF INTERVIEWS HELD AND OF OBSERVATION CARRIED OUT IN THE CHURCHES OF ST. GEORGE'S

F. CYRIL LAMONTAGNE

- Was born in St. Lucia; 55 years old–diocesan with around 16 years in Grenada—General Vicar of the diocese.

- He explains that in St. Vincent, Barbados, and Antigua most of the believers belong to the Anglican and Methodist Churches, while in the French West Indies, as in the Spanish ones, the majority are Catholic. Grenada keeps the Catholic predominance of the colonial period under France, which has also culturally left other marks.

- He establishes a difference between the massive level of participation, which includes attendance to Sunday mass, and the intense participation, which is by a minority. His view is that in Grenada the levels of attendance to the Historical Protestant churches are close to those of Catholicism: more intense during the festivities—Christmas, Holy Week, Lent.

- As to the liturgy, he says that there are several priests trying to assimilate the reforms of the Vatican II.

- On being asked about his opinion regarding the theology of liberation, and in general regarding this renewed line of thought, he answered that Grenada is not a country with a large concentration of wealth; that there are neither the very rich nor the extremely poor; that there is a predmoninance of a poverty characterized by a low standard of living, but not by misery (only in unusual cases); he adds that attendance to church is representative of this composition, and that he thinks this specific fact makes a theology of liberation that would adjust to other realities to be less adequate in the country. These observations follow his doubts about the strictly theological character of these theories.

- Composition of the clergy by countries: at present there are only 2 Grenadian priests and another four from the West Indies; there are 16 Irish, British Canadians and Americans, which complete the present 22 priests.

- In the '70s three priests were brought from Nigeria with the aim of increasing the proportion of blacks, but he says this experience was a fialure because they did not have a good adaptation and that 2 of them left, and the third one will soon go back to Nigeria. They chose Nigeria because of the experience and contacts of the Kiltegan friars there.

- On assessing negative reactions on the part of the clergy to social change in Grenada, he puts them down to the difficulties of the transition from a church that rules to a church that serves. He centers the problems on the European clergy whom he thinks should proportionally decrease in years ahead in favour of an indigenous clergy from the regions.

- The Catholic Episcopal Conference (West Indies) has two major seminaries: one in Trinidad and another in Jamaica. Both seminaries are—diocesan and the former now has around 20 seminarists, while the latter has around 10. They are affiliated to the University of the West Indies (UWI) so that their level would fit to that what is tought—there and the degree confered would be correspondent.

- He explains the dependence of the West Indian dioceses on the Congregation for the Evangelization of the Peoples and the Propagation of the Faith instead of on the Congregation of Bishops, like in the rest of America, due to financial reasons. The Caribbean Church is not able to finance itself and subordination to the above Congregation assures its financing as the region is considered a territory of Mission.

- He points out that the relations Church-State under Gairy were not easy, but that the Church managed to keep its status because the government knew its social influence. He adds that the Church has to show its capacity to carry out its mission beyond the ideologies being predominant in society.

- He said that at present the Church does not object the changes by the PRG, but that it has critical apprisals. He understands that there have been mistakes both by the PRG leadership and the Church. In the Church the foreign clergy is not as able as to understand the internal questions and reacts hastily, adopting wrong positions. The PRG has interpreted these positions as being those of the Church, but it has been made clear that those manifestations do not express the position of the Church.

- In spite of maintaining these criteria, he admitted that the statement by the journalist Alister Hughes in the Congress of the DFP of Dominica, summoning the Church to exert pressure on the public opinion around this question, was not an appropriate channel; and he says that this is not the Church's position. He recognizes that out of the 400 initial prisoners, over 75% have been set free, and that in this shows that the PRG has not acted intransigently in this sense.

- He is interested in knowing whether Marxism necessarily assumes atheism and whether we understand the building of Socialism as conditioned by atheistic positions. He has the opinion that in the Island (I think he means the political leadership without expressly affirming it) there is the view that religious faith and Socialism are not compatible and that they are willing to accept Socialism as long as one does not start from this criterion of incompatibility. He stresses that he is, above all and first of all, a man of the Church and that he will always react as such, but that he is willing to accept, within this framework, a Socialist transformation. That the Church would also have to facilitate the assimiliation of these changes for the believers.

● He asks questions on Cuba, the Church, the training of the clergy (whether there is a major seminary, whether it is integrated to the higher education system, etc.). He says he is interested in visiting Cuba, but that he does not know in what way this visit could take place.

OPINION:

Lamontagne is, as he said, a man of the Church, representative of the positions of the institution. In my opinion, he cannot be evaluated as a progressive clergyman, but as one who could assimilate a Church within the framework of radical social transformations. I think that his willingness to visit Cuba and his interest in doing so should not be underestimated because he visit could contribute, on the one hand, to counteract the effects of propaganda schemes; on the other, it would help in differentiating his situation within the clergy of the diocese . . .

6. PROPAGANDA AND PUBLIC RELATIONS IN THE USA

This section includes some of the most politically interesting of the Grenada documents. Throughout the life of the NJM regime, continuing efforts were made to influence American opinion through friendly Congressmen and 'staffers', and the media. Particularly striking are revelations of extensive contacts between Members of Congress and Communist leaders, within the United States as well as internationally. In view of the entitlement of Congressmen to classified information within the intelligence and security agencies and in the Pentagon, the documents disclose a hitherto unsuspected security risk for the US Administration.

Letter on Grenadian Dissidents
16 May 1980

As this and other documents in this section make clear, a key role in Grenada's public relations with the United States was played by the office of Ronald V. Dellums, a (black) Representative (Democrat, California). The writer of the document below was Dessima Williams, Grenada's Ambassador to the Organisation of American States (OAS). Barbara Lee was on Congressman Dellums's staff. The subject of the Ambassador's letter is an anti-PRG (People's Revolutionary Government, as the New Jewel Movement regime styled itself) propaganda leaflet which, to the writer's evident bafflement, had been stamped from the Prime Minister's office and postmarked in Grenada.

110

Telex: 64528   Telephone: (202) 265–2561

PERMANENT MISSION OF GRENADA TO THE ORGANIZATION OF AMERICAN STATES
Suite 203 – 1424 Sixteenth St., N.W. Washington, D.C. 20036
Tel. 347–3198

TO: Cde. Minister of National Security—Bishop
FROM: Cde. Ambassador Williams
DATE: May 16, 1980
RE: The attached mailing from Prime Minister's Office

Comrade:

On May 14, 1980, Barbara Lee called to say she had received a piece of anti-PRG propaganda stamped from the Prime Minister's Office, post-marked in Grenada. We collected it May 15, and it is herewith attached [excerpt annexed below].

Some obvious questions are:- What concerns us is: How is it possible for such vicious anti-government propaganda to be mailed and stamped from the Prime Minister's Office to a friendly Congressional Office?

Who?
How?

Barbara says that all those U.S. persons who went to Grenada for The First Anniversary have been receiving G.I.S. News Releases regularly. Should this be so? To her knowledge, no one else except she has received this particular piece of anti-PRG material.

. . . .

Please advise us at an early time if this was a known or unknown error; if a conspiracy and/or sabotage, and how to handle it.

Neither, 'Shampoo' Norbert Douglas our Security Officer at the Mission here, nor I have a clue on this. Only speculations:

[signature]
DESSIMA WILLIAMS

ANNEX: "BISHOP AND HIS COMMUNIST NEW JEWEL GANG"

. . . .

BRIEF SUMMARY OF OPPRESSIVE ACTS ALREADY TAKEN BY BISHOP'S COMMUNIST ILLEGAL REGIME IN GRENADA

In the exercise of unauthorised absolute power there are no limits and Bishop and his Communist New Jewel are already guilty of the following acts: Terrorism (illegally and violently seizing power, and causing extreme fear among the people), Treason (disloyalty to the sovereign in order to compel change of policy) Murder (giving guns to untrained youths to kill themselves and paying others to kill) Setting up missile bases all over Grenada with the help of Cuba, and putting guns everywhere in Grenada, imprisonment of hundreds of people in Grenada without trial, including Ministers, Leaders of Opposition parties, Doctors, Lawyers, students, and cancellation of visiting rights of families and friends, seizing of people's property (house, car etc) after arrest and imprisonment, seizure of the privately owned Cocoa Cola Factory, Evening Palace Club, other private homes, etc: closing down the only non-governmental newspaper 'The Torchlight', closing the courts, revoking all recognized laws and substituting their own laws with twice yearly trial by tribunal comprising of people with no legal background, serious violations of all humans rights and freedoms, prevention of people from leaving Grenada (scholarship holders and any one suspected of being a threat to the revolution), tapping of all telephones in Grenada and censoring of all mails, etc entering and leaving Grenada, importation of Cuban doctors and other personnel to take over jobs held by Grenadians, sending people without passports for training in Cuba and bringing in another personnel from Cuba under the guise of exchange program, detaining, searching and questioning and then imprisoning anyone arriving in Grenada who is known or even suspected to be a family or friend of any member of Gairy's party or any one in custody.

. . . .

Letter from Carlottia Scott to Maurice Bishop (pages 114–15) 28 April 1982

A particularly revealing document. Carlottia Scott, an aide to Congressman Dellums (see previous document), referred to as 'Ron' in her letter. Ms Scott describes Dellums's impressions after his first trip to Grenada. Note references to Fidel Castro.

Congress of the United States
House of Representatives
Washington, D.C. 20515

April 28, 1982

My Dearest,

Just a brief note to let you know that I still love you madly. However, I won't go
into that at this particular time. I really need to talk to you face to face to
share some thoughts that Ron has. I don't know if you realized it or not but Ron
has become truly committed to Grenada and has some very positive political thinking
to share with you. He feels that he can best be of assistance in a counseling manner
and hopes to be able to discuss these thoughts in the near furture. He just has to
get all to his thoughts in order as to how your interests can best be served. Ron,
as a political thinker, is the best around and Fidel will verify that in no uncertain
terms. When matched against the best of them, Ron always comes out ahead (even with
Fidel). He is so far ahead of his time that it scares me at times but I have learned
to deal with it over the years.

When we left Grenada and arrived in Barbados, we met with what I would call a very
ugly American, Ludlow Flowers, the Deputy Ambassador to B'dos from the U.S. In the
most awesome exchange of dialogue, Ron battled this ass to the bitter end on U.S.
policy toward Grenada. You would have been proud. Following that exchange, Ron vowed
to turn this Administration policy around. We are now in the process of pulling together the report for the Armed Services Committee, preparing testimony for the
Inter-American Affairs Committee Hearings on Grenada, and in the process of trying to
come up with a strategy to bring the U.S. and Grenada to the negotiating table. We
hope that this report will serve as a basis for a clear understanding and direct
counter to the Administration's policy based on their militarist lines of thinking. If
the issue can be turned around and soon, then we hope that all this insane rhetoric
will be stopped by the U.S. However, the specifics need to be mapped out very carefull
This is only part of what Ron needs to discuss with you in a much as this has to
be a team effort. (smile) Ron also has some very clear ideas on the best procedure
that should be followed on your end if you agree to proceed in such a manner. Oh
well, I won't bore you with all this until we are able to sit down and really discuss
it. It is really very very hard to put into a coherent statement at this time. As you
are well aware I act on emotion a lot of the time and I am very excited about the
role that Ron is willing to play after trying to get him to Grenada for so long. I
know now that all our efforts have not been in vain. Ron had a long talk with Barb and
me when we got to Havana and cried when he realized that we had been shouldering
Grenada alone all this time. Like I said, he's really hooked on you and Grenada and
doesn't want anything to happen to building the Revo and making it strong. He really
admires you as a person and even more so as a leader with courage and foresight, princ
and integrity. Believe me, he doesn't make that kind of statement often about anyone.
The only other person that I know of that he expresses such admiration for is Fidel.
(I've known and worked with Ron for many years and the last time I heard him say someth.
like that was in 1977 after a meeting with Fidel).

Well sweet, I must run. Am doing this as quickly as possible. Just found out that Kojo
(Chris) is leaving in a few minutes for the airport. I just wanted you to know that we
need to talk and soon. Am sending copies of Ron hearings with him. You will be receivi
a formal letter of appreciation for the wonderful trip from Ron soon. (As soon as I
get around to writing it, (SMILE) but I have to finish this report first.) For the r

I really need Selwyn's speech to use in this report. Peggy said he had the tape and it had not been transcribed yet. Please see if he has found it yet. It could be very important. Even if we don't use it for the report we could use it for the testimo for the hearings on Grenada in May.

Love you madly and hope to be able to prove it one of these days. Call me soon. (I can't afford to call until late next month. My phone bill was $300.00 last month) Give my love to everyone and tell Shaheba everyone sends their best.

Later,

CAWS

P.S. This is confidential rap as you will know. Let me know when you or one of the comrades will be taking a trip some where in this hemisphere so we can talk. Notice I said this hemisphere so we can plan to meet & talk. Call me.

North American Resistance Programme
29 March 1983

As shown by this unsigned document, the NJM regime had a wide network of friends and supporters in the USA who worked effectively to influence, and as far as possible mobilise, public opinion. Two aspects of this campaign, as revealed in the document below, are of special interest. One was the co-ordination of the campaign with the Sandinista regime of Nicaragua through the United Nations Security Council. The other is the reference (under 'Area 1', item 7) to 'C.P. Comrade Jackson'. James E. Jackson was an official of the Soviet-line Communist Party USA. Further on (under 'Washington') there is a reference to a better-known American Communist, Angela Davis, who was much to the fore during the Vietnam War in opposing US involvement and praising the Vietnamese Communists.

TO: POLITICAL BUREAU
DATE: NEW YORK, WEDNESDAY MARCH 29th, 1983
SUBJECT: INTERIM REPORT ON NORTH AMERICAN
           RESISTANCE PROGRAMME

Generally speaking, Grenada's fight-back campaign in North America has got off the ground. In terms of the four zones, New York is moving well; Washington has made a start; and in concrete preparations to step up their programme by Thursday. The West Coast got off the ground yesterday.

Consistent with the 26 point plan, our objectives are as follows:

1. To mobilize public opinion (including in Congress) in order to restrain the U.S. Government from attacking Grenada militarily;

2. To win long-term contacts and sympathy for Grenada, hence turning attacks to our advantage;

3. To solicit concrete assistance: paper, tape recorders, typewriters, etc.

As you know, Reagan attacked Grenada on national T.V. and radio just as I was about to arrive, showing spy photographs of our airport. We responded the very night and the response was carried on radio, but no widely in the media.

Grenada's address to the Security Council the next day evoked some interest. Many journalists (NBC, TIME, etc.) interviewed Caldwell after his speech, in which he spent five minutes on Grenada, but we have not seen or heard anything come out, except on radio. In fact, minutes after requesting interviews, many T.V. stations changed their minds saying, they "can't find crew". Clearly the word was to, "blank Grenada".

I understand that a few blacks and liberal whites used their influence and got ABC television to arrange the interview with Maurice. The airing of this interview has become the turning point. It is being released in bits. It's a road march. Previously, it was Reagan's speech that was the road march. According to Tom Wicker, N.Y. Times journalist on the David Brinkley (ABC) Show "This Week" Reagan has "lost credibility" for his phoney satellite pictures of Grenada since the airport is open to T.V. cameras. Brinkley agreed and they laughed. (Note that tens of millions view this show). Assistant Secretary of Defence, Ikle, embarrassed himself on National (ABC) T.V. "Night Line" with Ted Copple who shook him up brilliantly—tens of millions of viewers—trying to project Grenada as a threat and had to resort to "Russian style obstacle course", human rights, etc. He stated that unlike Haiti, our type of process is "irreversible".

[Illegible]

Reagan's speech was effective, but no very much so since the "Soviet military build-up" idea is so stale. We were in some "star wars" technology. Therefore, the statements on Grenada were hidden in proposals with far-reaching strategic implications. Of course, the photographs of Cuba, [Illeg.] ads being visual aids would have helped his case a little, but only a little. In the end, the administration looked a bit silly, with respect ot Grenada.

Over the past few hours, I note that they are trying to recoup the situation. The same ABC News has come up with a slanted version of the Grenada item, basically reversing themselves, stating that the airport will be used largely for Soviet aircraft, including Bear aircraft, especially since we have few hotel rooms. We have to respond to it. They're fighting back fiercely, using the same ABC but out of Washington this time. Very latest reports confirm that ABC has changed their line. They are now projecting Grenada as a threat, using the sea lanes and "Cuban troops to Angola" arguments. Our size is irrelevant, they say. They've bowed to State Department pressure.

(*Later changed again—second "ABC" Interview*)

. . . .

HERE ARE SOME OF THE ACTIVITIES—AREA BY AREA

(Areas are Washington/Atlanta/South: Dessima; North-East: Caldwell (plus Burke); West Coast: Ian; Canada: Benjie)

AREA 1 NEW YORK/DETROIT (BASE OF OPERATIONS)

1. Planning meeting with Grenada Ambassador and Ian, leaders of work in four zones.

2. Participation in Security Council debate on Nicaragua.

3. Meeting with U.N. Secretary-General. He listened attentively and appeared somewhat concerned.

4. Radio interviews: WLIB, WBAI (including Maurice's)

5. Meeting with hundred key Grenadians, leaders of organisations.

6. Press conference at U.N. Headquarters with large turnout of international press.

7. Meeting with C.P. Comrade Jackson. Party will give general support.

8. Meeting with leading white liberals, and progressive blacks, academics, media people, ANC and influential types. Best of its kind for years, over three hundred (double the number expected) attended, coming from all over the region.

9. Substantial Radio, T.V. and newspaper coverage of U.N. Press Conference by national media, ranging from skeptical to favourable, but mostly "balanced", quoting both sides together.

10. Biggest event is rally planned for next Sunday April 3, in New York.

DETROIT (Burke)

Meeting with Caribbean organisations, Grenadians, Students, Press. As of yesterday, Tuesday, the situation with regional/national press/publicity was as follows:

— New York Times article (pg. 7)—Saturday.

— Daily Challenge (only Black national circulation of just over 100,000.)

— Short New York Times piece (Front page)—skeptical.

— WINS, most listened to radio station in New York area gave good reports.

— New York Daily News (Positive story of U.N. Press Conference on prominent position, large cirulation close to that of New York Times).

— Daily Challenge again.

— Short story in Wall St. Journal: Front page (from press conference).

— As mentioned earlier, ABC interview with Maurice showing airport in favourable light until the recent twist.

— Large number of radio interviews.

— Small number of short T.V. clips of press conference.

MOOD OF GRENADIANS (GENERAL)

Our nationals are in high spirits. Reagan's attack on their airport has firmed them up. This is true in the U.S., Canada and Britain. We invited seventy-five (75) carefully chosen Grenadians to brief them on their tasks for Sunday's rally and a little over a hundred turned up, inspite of hours of heavy rain (and most didn't have transport). In little time, funds were raised for radio advertisements for the rally. Hundreds are phoning up all our missions expressing support. It is difficult to keep up with the noting of calls.

WASHINGTON (Dessima)

— A brief rap (five minutes) with a hundred leading progressives and Blacks (Angela Davis, PLO Rep., etc.) at a function.

— Half hour rap on Howard University Radio.

— Fascinating meeting with OAS Secretary-General Orfila. His response to Maurice's letter was sympathetic and supportive. "The Americans have closed the door on dialogue" he said. He went on to add that this makes him frustrated. He will meet right away with William Clarke, Reagan's National Security Advisor.

— An ABC T.V. interview on meeting with Orfila (fact of presenting letter, content etc.) has not been aired.

— Caribbean Ambassadors' Caucus. Guyana—supportive; Jamaica—sympathetic; Barbados—skeptical; Antigua—concerned, but in an idealistic way.

— Arrangements are being finalized for meeting with Congressional Black Caucus, Senators/Congressmen, rally, press conference, OAS protocolary session.

CALIFORNIA (Ian)

Tuesday 29th—(1) Interview with Radio, T.V., two newspapers. (2) Meeting with Friendship Society. (3) Address to Oakland City Council with possibility of solidarity resolution being passed later in week.

Wednesday 30th—Major press conference due (Note difference in time) The U.N. Press Conference was front page in San Francisco Chronicle, largest circulation paper in region. Balanced report.

The publicity is also preparing ground, whipping up interest in build-up for Sunday's rally with Dessima, Claudette Pitt etc.

U.K. (Dennis)

— Meeting in Sheffield. Fifty persons—Firm.
— Letters delivered.

—Met with Minister Cranley Enslow* who said that this is a figment of our imagination and that he will respond in writing. He also said we've stopped relaying BBC news.

— Demonstration planned in front of U.S. Embassy on Tuesday, first working day after long weekend.

— Black media briefed.

— Large media resisting access to us.

. . . .

OVERVIEW

All in all, the programme is taking shape and we are getting reasonable responses and results. So far tens of millions would have got our version (ABC has a high rating and David Brinkley's "This Week" report and "Night Line" are listened to by tens of millions.) In addition to the news, there have been more than a dozen radio interviews. Many of the radio stations and newspapers reach over a million persons. Also, the attacks (and fightback) have widened and deepened our support and sympathy and the awareness of our situation among progressives, academics and Blacks. We are making progress on building a wider network of friends and allies vital for our future work.

. . . .

*At that time, the Cranley Onslow (corrected), MP, was Minister of State at the Foreign and Commonwealth Office.

Report on USA
April 1983

This detailed Report was written by Ian Jacobs, a special assistant to Bishop, in preparation for the NJM leader's US tour in the Spring of 1983. As in other documents, there are references to the special role of Barbara Lee, an aide to Representative Dellums. There are also references to the CPUSA and to the Socialist Workers' Party, an American Trotskyist group.

INTERIM REPORT ON NORTH AMERICA FROM
MARCH 23,—April 21, 1983

BY IAN JACOBS

I. INTRODUCTION:

It will be recalled that the explicit purpose of this visit was to assist in a campaign to counter attack President Reagan's verbal attack on Grenada high-lighted by his speeches of March [illeg.] and 23rd 1983. During my stay I visited eight cities in the U.S.A. and without hesitation I would say that the visit as a whole was a success, I make this assertion for the following reasons:

a) There was excellent media coverage—see section two of this report and appendix for sample news clippings.

b) Our North American networks once again proved their worth with excellent short notice organizational efforts.

c) Because of the above we were able to reach thousands of Americans with our message.

d) I anticipate that with the contracts that were made we should be able to raise between three to five thousand U.S. dollars—a figure that should allow us to purchase a word processor within three to six months.

II. [illeg.] OF VISIT:

A. March 23—28: Briefings in New York and Washington with Cdes. Whiteman, Taylor, Williams and Angela Davis.

B. March 29—April 2: Visit to California with stops in San Francisco, Oakland, Berkeley and Sacramento. During this stay there were [illeg.] activities as follows:

1. March 29—Oakland and Berkeley:

a) Live radio interview with K.P.F.A.—public radio station in Berkeley with a liberal [illeg.].

b) Interviews with People's World—newspaper of C.P.U.S.A.

2. March 30—Oakland, Berkeley and San Francisco:

a) Phone interview with K.A.L.X.—Berkeley campus radio station.

b) Phone interview with K.S.O.L.—most listened to black station in Oakland.

c) Phone interview with K.B.L.X.—second most listened to black station in Oakland.

d) Press conference at the San Francisco Press Club. Appearing with me was Angela Davis. Press present were the California voice, the Sun Reporter, Bay City wire service— the major regional wire service for the West Coast, Associated Press, Associated Press Radio, K.D.I.A. Radio—a black station, K.P.F.A.—public radio, K.A.L.X., Pacific Sun, K.R.O.N.—N.B.C. afiliate in San Francisco, the San Francisco N.A.A.C.P.

The conference went well with no major problems. The Press's main concern was my statement's reference to violations of our air and sea space.

e) Interview with the Oakland Tribune—Oakland's biggest paper which is also Black owned.

f) In the evening I gave a five minute address to the Oakland city council. I was politely received and one of the Black members (Wilson Ryles) moved a vote of thanks. However the original hope was that the council would pass a resolution in support of Grenada and calling for talks with the Reagan administration. This did not happen however because of poor advance groundwork by our comrades and the fact that the council is quite conservative. Added to this elections were due in three weeks.

3. March 31—Sacramento:

    a) Press conference at City Hall. Appearing with me were representatives of the Sacramento chapter of the U.S./Grenada Friendship Society. In attendance at the conference were representatives from the City's main media. Thus there were reporters from the Sacramento Bee—the city's main newspaper, the Sacramento Union—the city's second main newspaper, K.I.X.J. a city television station, K.C.R.A.—the city's main television station.

This conference went well but there were hostile questions from the reporter for K.C.R.A. This was not surprising as this city is viewed as quite conservative.

    b) Lunch hosted by the U.S./Grenada Friendship Society Chapter. The lunch was well attended with positive discussions highlighted by a commitment to get petitions sent to Washington and to raise funds for a world processing machine. There were some 40 people present representing various progressive groups such as N.B.I.P.P., S.C.L.C., N.A.A.C.P., Solidarity groups for El Salvador and Nicaragua. Also present were some Black businessmen.

    c) Interview with the editorial Board of the Sacramento Bee. This is supposed to be the liberal paper of Sacramento.

    d) Interview with the editor of the editorial page of the Sacramento Union. This is the more conservative paper in Sacramento but as the Appendix shows they gave more coverage to the visit.

4. April 1—Berkeley and Oakland:

    a) Meeting with the members of the Latin American division of the Political Science department of the Berkeley Campus of the University of California. This was essentially a briefing session for sympathetic students and faculty.

b) Lunch organised by the Oakland Chapter of the U.S./ Granada Friendship Society.

c) The Black Caucus agreed to pass a resolution in support of Grenada and send it to Washington. In discussions with Barbara Lee on April 20, 1983 she informed me that his had been done and a copy would be sent to us in Grenada.

d) The Black Caucus agreed to circulate a resolution in support of Grenada within the wider assembly and to send this resolution with as many signatures as possible to Washington. On April 20, 1983 Barbara Lee informed me that this resolution is presently circulating.

e) The Black Caucus agreed to visit Grenada in August 1983, with the group being organised by Barbara Lee.

7. April 7 and 8: Los Angeles:

With Extensive Assistance from the National Conference of Black Lawyers and the L.A. chapter of the U.S./Grenada Friendship Society we had a good visit to L.A. with the following activities:

On the evening of the 7th a dinner was held to welcome me. Sponsored by the N.C.B.I., N.B.I.P.P. and the L.A. chapter of the U.S./ Grenada Friendship Society, the dinner was well attended. There were representatives from the Southern Christian Leadership Conference (S.C.L.C.), N.B.I.P.P., C.P.U.S.A., A.N.C., Anti-Apartheid Committee, N.C.B.L. and the National Lawyers Guild. [illeg.] The main outcome of this event was a commitment by this group to help with getting copies of the pro Grenada resolution to Washington (See Appendix), and a commitment to raise funds for the Word Processor project.

The following events took place on the 8:

a) Interview with the Executive editor of the L.A. Sentinel—the leading Black newspaper in L.A.

b) Press conference at the L.A. Press Club. Appearing with me were representatives from the N.B.I.P.P. and the National Lawyers Guild. The conference was not badly covered with representatives from the L.A. Times, Channel 18 T.V.— local station, People's World, Voice of the People and Cable Network News—C.N.N.—national station. There was no conflict but the main questions dealt with the location and size of the counter revolutionary force.

c) Radio interview with K.J.L.H.—the leading Black radio station in L.A.

d) Radio interview with K.P.F.K.—the public radio station in L.A.

e) Reception hosted by the N.C.B.I. and the National Lawyers Guild. The representation of people at this function was very wide with Liberal, Progressive, Black Nationalist and Peace Interests all represented. The total number of people was about 75 and there was a commitment to assist with the resolution as well as to raise funds for the Word Processor project.

8. April 13—19: Miami and Washington:

This last period was largely spent in Miami with a visit to Washington for funds and consultations with Cde. Dessima Williams. The visit to Miami was very successful as the following was achieved:

a) live radio interview with [illeg.] an all news station in Miami with a wide listenership. There was a phone-in section and the calls were about 50% in favour of our position. The show lasted one hour.

b) Phone-in interview with the National Black Network news service. This service serves the Black community nation-wide. The interview lasted ten minutes.

c) Newspaper interview with the Miami News, Miami's main evening paper owned by Miami Herald. The interview was quite warm but the article that resulted from the interview (see Appendix) contained some inaccuracies.

d) Newspaper interview with the Miami Herald, Miami's main newspaper. The interviewer was [illeg.] who has been to Grenada a few times and Juan Tamayo. Basically the inter-view was friendly but they said from the outset that they would print nothing unless I had information on the size of the counter revolutionary force and its exact location.

e) a press conference was held with fairly good coverage. [illeg.] present was A.B.C. (their Miami affiliate), N.B.C. (their Miami affiliate), W.I.N.Z.—an all news station with a wide listenership.

f) A phone-in interview with W.G.B.S. an all news and talk station with a wide cross section of listeners. This lasted for five minutes.

g) A taped radio interview with the Haitian Refugee Centre. They have a one hour program every week on a Miami station and this interview would be used for that program. The inter-view went well as they were supportive.

h) A live radio interview on W.N.N.S. an all news station which claims to have a listenership to this particular program (a regular talk and phone-in show) of between two and three hundred thousand people. The program lasted three hours and the phone-in segment was about 50% in our favor. Appearing to counter my presentation was [illeg.], a Grenadian counter living in Miami. He was friendly but very blatant in his lies about our revolution. He is obviously well financed in Miami as he runs a well produced (although full of lies) newspaper which he distributes free. He also drives a luxury American car (1983 model) and lives in an exclusive area of Miami. A copy of the paper has been supplied to Cde. Bishop with his copy of this report.

i) There was a public meeting held at the Chalet Centre in the middle of Liberty City, that well known Black area (the riots of 1981—82) of Miami. The meeting was covered by the Miami Herald and [illeg.] (regional station). There were about 150 people present (three Grenadians—Troy Garvey, Carol Peterson and Sally [illeg.] Smith) and generally it was a good meeting with positive support. Apart from outlining the present situation I also used the opportunity to circulate the resolution on Grenada (see Appendix). One point to note was that although the meeting was held in Liberty City, only about 10–20 blacks were at the meeting.

j) I had a meeting with Mr. Aaron Schecter, a wealthy Jew who is very supportive of the Peace Movement. The idea was to get a commitment for a contribution to the Word Processor project. He agreed to contribute (somewhere between U.S. $1,000—2,000) if I would get a tax credit organised for him. To do this his contribution would have to go to a tax exempt organisation. In this context I spoke to a contact at the American Friends Service Committee in Philadelphia and I intend to follow up with them so that he can send the money to them and then they will send it here.

While the visit to Miami was overall quite successful it must be pointed out that this was inspite of the S.W.P. [Socialist Workers Party] Miami branch which tried desperately to seize the visit for their own purposes. Had this happened we would not have reacheed so wide a cross section of people but fortunately they were outmaneuovred by both myself and the local organisation that really put together the visit—[illeg.]—a broad front organisation that concentrates on support for anti-imperialist forces in Latin and Central America.

. . . .

The visit's success was due to the ground work of some key people and some key organisations. Among them are:

A. The West Coast:

 1. Angela and Fonja Davis.

 2. Gus Newport [Mayor of Berkeley, CA].

 3. Barbara Lee.

 4. The National Conference of Black Lawyers.

 5. The National Lawyers Guild.

 6. The National Black Independence Political Party.

 7. The U.S./Grenada Friendship Society branches in Berkeley, Oakland, San Francisco and Sacramento.

B. Philadelphia:

 1. The American Friends Service Committee.

 2. Freddy Hill—Professor at Haverford College in Haverford Pennsylvania.

C. Miami:

 1. The La Casa Group.

IV. IDEAS FOR FOLLOW UP:

A. Funds for the Word Processor project. These should come from L.A. and Miami mainly.

B. The California Legislator's Resolutions on Grenada should arrive soon from Barbara Lee. Also the visit of the Black Caucus from the California legislator should be followed up with Barbara Lee. This visit is planned for August.

C. The resolution campaign should be monitored so as to make sure it takes place. The key person here is Fonja Davis.

V. CONCLUSIONS

This particular visit was undoubtedly a success. The efforts of our organisation on the ground in the various cities is a key reason for that success. At the same time however, it is clear that there is much sympathy for Grenada (particularly in the black community and among liberal and progressive Whites), a sympathy advanced by Reagan's hostility. Thus I think it is correct to [illeg.] that we must continue to tap that pro Grenada sentiment [illeg.] of North Americans with a properly organised [illeg.]. A broad and continuous propaganda campaign that always keeps our revolution in the minds of North America. From my experience this means that our missions must organise a year round propaganda campaign that includes:

a) The proper and regular distribution of news on the Revolution throughout North America.

b) Planned visits by Embassy officials to various parts of North America. Of particular value here would be Embassy involvement on the Campus circuit—i.e. regular appearance at University Campuses for payment of a fee.

c) Close links with important progressive movements like the peace movement in particular.

d) Regular visits from top P.R.G. officials to North America.

Certainly not all of these things are happening now, but I would suggest that unless they do (and undoubtedly other activities too) we will lose the momentum we have and more importantly we will lose a constituency that is vital in our battles against U.S. imperialism.

IAN JACOBS
APRIL 27, 1983

Advice on US Tour

Further advice on Bishop's US tour came Gail Reed, US-born wife of the Cuban Ambassador to Grenada, Julian Torres Rizo (a former

*head of the UN station of the Cuban intelligence service, the
Dirección General de Inteligencia or DGI). This letter, undated, was
handwritten in the original. Of special interest is Reed's advice to
Bishop to work out the agenda for his proposed meetings in the United
States with Parodi, of the Cuban Interests Section which, in the
absence of formal diplomatic relations between Havana and
Washington, is the official Cuban diplomatic representation in the
US.*

Dear Maurice—

I've given some thought to what you raised over the phone, and come
up with a couple of ideas, although without [illeg.] the general picture of
what the trip looks like and perspectives you have on it—a big limi-
tation. But for what it's worth:

1) I think being pressured into coming up with a major announce-
ment, declaration, etc. or even a gimmick along these lines is a bit of a
trap. [illeg.] With all due respect to the power of the U.S. media, once
you've got their attention, the agenda must be yours, not theirs.
Although I haven't been in the States recently, certain things don't
change: the U.S. media go after violence, and when there's no war, con-
troversy will due just as well—especially in an election year. I would
say they're most interested in the visit as it fits in to their idea of a
"faceoff" with Reagan and his administration, in the midst of the election campaign. But, of course, Grenada's interests are far different.
And it seems to me the best idea is to stick with those interests and
objectives, and use the media as far as possible to advance them, [illeg.]
without getting "cornered."

2) Why the visit? (Of course, you've given the answer to this one
more thought than I.) But for the media, how does this sound:
"Grenada and the United States have a long history of relations—
many thousands of Grenadians live in the United States, their work
contributing to the development of that country; many thousands of
U.S. citizens travel to Grenada to enjoy its hospitality and natural
beauty; cultural similarities united Grenada with cultural currents in
the U.S.; other economic links, etc., etc. The purpose of the visit is to
reaffirm and develop these ties at as many levels as possible, and by so
doing to help lessen the tensions that have cropped up at one of these

levels: the current White House administration [illeg.]." Thus, the importance of accepting the Black Caucus (*another governmental level*) and Transafrica invitations—as *important in themselves*—leaving open the possibility of meeting with the Reagan administration if it were to come off.

I think any suggestion that accepting these invitations is really a "cover" for another (larger) purpose (such as a meeting with Reagan) needs to be denied flatly, and strongly. After all, what is contained in the suggestion, besides the implication that the PRG is opportunist, is the *racist* and *anti-popular* implication—"why would he come here just because a bunch of Black folks invited him?"

The strong answer is that *of course* it is legitimate in its own right—to speak directly to *the people*, to other levels of their government, etc. That is *what the PRG is all about.*

3) I still think it might be a good idea to launch the organizing of the "US-Grenada Friendship Flight" (or some such *better* name), the inaugural flight direct to Grenada's new international airport for March 13th. Beyond a tourism boost, I think it would go a long way to promote the "open-ness of Grenada and its airport to U.S. citizens," as well as the idea that the airport is a normal one, a good thing for U.S. travellers too. Over time, the flight itself could be a focus for publicity—of the important figures that will be on board, the Grenadians going home. (Wouldn't the medical school like to donate cash for a few seats so "prize trips" could be awarded, let's say, to a [illeg.] Grenadian [illeg.] couple from New York, a trade unionist from Detroit?—Anyway, that's just a thought for the future.)

4) On the specific meetings, I think I'm too out of touch to be helpful. [Illeg.] Parodi from the Cuban Interests Section will be the single most clear person on this whole question. (Only comment: I think the contact with Gil Noble is important.)

Reading this over, it's pretty rambling, but I hope of some use.

By the way—the ABC interview was beautiful!

Take care of yourself.
Warm regards,
Gail

Background Notes for Meeting with
National Security Adviser Clark

One of the most important meetings arranged for Bishop was to be with the White House National Security Adviser, Judge William P. Clark (spelt 'Clarke' in the document below). This set of notes, unsigned and undated, but presumably for the guidance of Maurice Bishop, suggested that the NJM leader should take the initiative, 'even perhaps the offensive' during the meeting.

BRIEFING NOTES ON MEETING WITH JUDGE WILLIAM CLARKE, CHAIRMAN OF THE N.S.C.

Section—1: Background on the N.S.C.:

Originally the N.S.C. had been an advisory board on Foreign Policy. However under Nixon (with Kissinger as Chairman of the N.S.C.) and Carter (with Brezinski as Chairman of the N.S.C.) and now Reagan the council has become a key body in the formulation of U.S. foreign policy.

Indeed it is now widely felt (certainly in the Washington Post and Time Magazine) that the N.S.C. under Clarke has become the chief formulator of U.S. foreign policy. Certainly this is evident in recent U.S. foreign policy decisions in Central America where it is widely felt that the removal of Enders (under Secretary of State for Latin American Affairs) and Hinton (Ambassador to El Salvador) is linked directly to Clarke's recommendations. Signficantly it is also widely felt that Clarke (together with Jane Kirkpatrick at the U.N.) is the real formulator of policy in Latin America and the Caribbean.

While this is an apparent reality it should be noted that Clarke has absolutely no background in foreign affairs at all. His only credential is his close friendship to Reagan. Moreover that friendship is based on a shared hard line right wing approach on everything including his limited knowledge on foreign affairs.

This dichotomy of control and limited knowledge has led to much conflict between the N.S.C. and the State Department where more real knowledge on foreign affairs exists. Nevertheless it is clear that for now the National Security Council under Clarke is calling most if not all of the shots on foreign policy, particularly in regards to central America and Caribbean.

Section II: Talking Notes

1. Comrade Bishop must clearly in practice and also been seen to take the initiative, even perhaps the offensive in the meeting. Two main reasons:

1. We asked for the meeting, so we must demonstrate that we have issues, topics, and agenda.

2. The psycological struggle will be fierce, but, of course, very sophisticated. We must definitely win that struggle.

Section III: Suggested proposals:

Concretely propose the following:

1. Our two countries must exchange Ambassadors this year, 1983.

2. The United States Government must end its economic aggression and propaganda destabilization against Grenada without delay.

Later These two points will be added:

1. Miami-based agents of destabilization

2. Cease your support for countries—those opposed to PRG and extradite Gairy.

Section IV: Background on Grenada's Position:

For over three (3) years, Grenada's PRG has been saying we want to normalize diplomatic relations with the United States:

—Bernard Coard to Pete Vaky, Carter's Assistant Secretary of States to Inter-American Affairs

—In almost every multilateral forum e.g. OAS, CARICOM, UN.

—Cde. Whiteman has also made the point on all of his visits here

At the same time the U.S. has refused to respond to many of our overtures.

Handwritten Minutes of Meeting with
National Security Adviser Clark
(No date)

These minutes of Bishop's meeting with National Security Adviser Clark are undated and unsigned, although probably drafted by Grenada's Ambassador to the OAS, Dessima Williams. The reference to 'Mittendorf' is presumably to the American Ambassador to the OAS, William J. Middendorf II.

NOTES OF BISHOP MEETING
WITH JUDGE CLARKE

We must *protest* the meeting not occurring as we were led to believe—

—Long delay

—Mittendorf the chief host

Clark, Dam, Mittendorf, Bosch, Browne

M. Glad for meeting, been requesting it for some time.

—Need to start off on the long history of good people to people relations.

Bottom line: dialogue and normal relations

—Commision: a Discuss differences

b Discuss cooperation

Clarke—No problems with dialogue, more interested in conduct

Concerned with Soviet influence among our neighbors

Soviet influence in region is not acceptable

Can communicate to you our response to your proposals

Agreed to off the record meeting a secret meeting

Not only to refer to this meeting

Expect change in criticisms in future.

Have common strands (history)—legal practice. Hope this can lead to great progress.

M.—Encouraged by his response—that they are willing to accept talks on the normalization of relations.

—Our language (careful) should [be] noted

—toning down of attacks must be mutual

Clarke Their preference is to sit around the table re discussions rather [than] public attacks.

Referred to moving location of the school—not for this conference

Hope that we return to basic form of govt. rather than model of E. Eur.

Judge's departure

M. Time perspective re reply to our pro[posals?]

Dam—Key thing is Sov./Cuban influence

Need to see some change in conduct before the agreement

M.—Will have to look at econ. destabl.

C.D.B., IMF.

—Tourism re res[?]

—We can explore any range of subjects and give fullest assurance that we constitute no threat to the US

Dam—Interested in assurances

"Thank you for coming to meet with Judge Clarke."

—Re shift in venue

—Length of time judge stayed

—Points he made

—Tone/atmosphere

—State Dept. component (Dam)

—Meaning of the press/press state[ment?]

7. THE LEADERSHIP STRUGGLE

In all communist parties without exception, whether in power or in opposition, struggles for power take place between factions and their leaders. The New Jewel Movement was no exception to this rule. The difference between it and the better-known or much larger parties is that the NJM faction struggles are now in the public domain because of the discovery of the Grenada documents.

Although communist leaders tend to stay in power, or in control of their parties, much longer than the leaders of parties competing for popular support in democratic societies, they can be and sometimes are removed—not by a popular vote, but when outmanoeuvred by their rivals within the party machine.

Thus the former Soviet party boss, Nikita Khrushchev, mustered support within the CPSU's Central Committee to oust the rivals who were trying to oust him in 1957: especially Molotov and Malenkov. Having lost the fight, Khrushchev's ousted colleagues were dubbed the 'anti-party group'. In 1964, however, it was Khrushchev's turn to be removed in a typical palace coup, in favour of Leonid Brezhnev.

In microcosm, the same kind of thing happened within the Grenadian NJM, as shown by the documents in this section. We reproduce two of the crucial texts: the minutes of the extraordinary meeting of the NJM's Central Committee held on Friday 15 October 1982, at which the resignation from both the Political Bureau and the Central Committee was announced; and the minutes of the meeting of the Political Bureau a year later, on 12 October 1983, from which it is clear that Coard was now in the ascendant and Bishop on his way out. Four days later, Bishop was arrested in Coard's coup.

Typically, the differences between the Coard and Bishop factions are expressed in the coded language of Leninism. Thus at the 1982 meeting, the decision to accept Coard's resignation was taken in the name of 'democratic centralism'. Coard had let it be known that he had decided to resign six months previously on the grounds that his authority as Chairman of the OC (Organisation Committee) was being undermined and that there was a general failure to implement major decisions. It appears that although Coard had resigned, he subsequently secured the removal from the Central Committee of two of Bishop's allies, Vincent Noel and Kenrick Radix. Coard was clearly biding his time. A year later, taking advantage of a prolonged absence abroad by Maurice Bishop (always a mistake in a threatened leader), Coard mustered the support he needed. Back from State visits to Czechoslovakia and Hungary, and an unscheduled stop in Havana, Bishop found the tide had turned against him.

Central Committee Meeting
15 October 1982

MINUTES OF THE EXTRA-ORDINARY MEETING OF THE CENTRAL COMMITTEE OF THE NJM NEW JEWEL MOVE-MENT—FRIDAY 15th OCTOBER, 1982

Present:

Maurice Bishop	Ewart Layne
George Louison	Phyllis Coard
Selwyn Strachan	Leon Cornwall
Unison Whiteman	Kamau McBarnette
Kenrick Radix	Caldwell Taylor
Hudson Austin	Fitzroy Bain
Liam James	Ian St. Bernard
Chalkie Ventour	Ian Bartholomew
	Chris DeRiggs

On Tuesday 12th October, 1982, the Central Committee of NJM was convened by CC Chairman Cde. Maurice Bishop in an extraordinary plenary to discuss a letter of resignation from Cde. Bernard Coard, Deputy Party Leader and to examine the issues raised in the letter related to the state of the Party and the crisis in the work of the higher organs.

Within the period of the meeting, the CC held four sessions totalling 32 hours. The crisis in the work of the higher organs was analysed, the performance of each member of the CC was assessed and a number of decisions on the way forward were taken.

Subsequent to two hours of initial deliberations, the CC settled on an approach to the meeting. Cde. Strachan was asked to summarize his discussions with Cde. Coard in relation to the matter of his resignation. Cde. Strachan made the following points:-

i) Cde. Coard had indicated that his decision to resign from PB and CC was taken 6 months previously;
ii) His decision to resign from CC was primarily on account of strain but this was hastened by certain developments—linked to this was the undermining of his authority as Chairman of the OC.
iii) He had made reference to the slackness of the CC and its unwillingness to speak up on issues, the lack of preparation for meetings by CC comrades, and the unwillingness of the CC to study.
iv) In order to take corrective action it would result in personality clashes with the Chairman of the CC.
v) His presence was a fetter to the development of the CC if viewed dialectically.
vi) His resignation is not negotiable.
vii) In the final analysis stringent Leninist measures are required.

The meeting also listened to what was explained to be the main theoretical options presented by Cde. Coard to the Central Committee:

i) His own resignation
ii) He remains and tolerates slackness of CC and PB

iii) Put all members of CC into work committees
iv) Expand the Political Bureau

The meeting moved to address itself to the issues raised by Cde. Coard in his conversationwith several CC members. Cde. Layne was asked to comment on resolutions and decisions taken by the Central Committee since April, 1981 relating to the introduction of Leninist measures in the Party. Cde. Layne pointed to the following:-

April, 1981: The resolution of the CC addressed itself to:-

    a. Tight chairmanship
b.   [word missing] application of high standards of discipline and self-critical approach by all committees
    c. The setting up of a Secretariat and appointment of Recording Secretaries.

September, 1981: Analysis was done on:-
    a. state of comrade's health
    b. lack of personal work plans

Decisions:-
    a. CC would meet once per month
    b. OC would draft schedule of rest for comrades
    c. CC members would do personal work plans

December, 1981:
    a. There was a lack of follow up work and a failure to implement major decisions.
    b. Information on decisions taken was not sent down to all levels of the Party.

April, 1982: The CC considered problems related to:-
    a. discipline
    b. study
    c. standards
    d. planning
    e. arrogance throughout the party
    f. work performance of members of the higher organs
    g. [word missing] of information

June, 1982: The OC analysis of the Party has indicated that:
  i) There was a collapse of nearly all areas of Party work, name:-

  a. workers
  b. youth
  c. women
  d. state

In this period the mood of the masses had been described as lower than May Day. The work of the OC had been described as bureaucratic and giving no guidance to work committees.

July, 1982: In discussing the present state of the Party, the following weaknesses were pointed out:-

  a. control mechanisms were not working
  b. there was looseness in Party organization
  c. activities were controlling the work of the CC
  d. a Party School was required for Party members to master the science of Marxism-Leninism

The CC agreed that there were certain recurring, glaring weaknesses:-
  i) the improper functioning of Central Committee and Political bureau
  ii) the lack of control at the level of Central Committee

Comrades also cited additional evidence of the crisis:-

  i) lack of collectivity in building the Party—few PB and CC comrades were giving serious thought to the work and this resulted in low levels of participation in the work;
  ii) PB and CC had been "ducking" the real issues;
  iii) there was dead weight at CC and PB level and this urgently had to be addressed;
  iv) the CC was not studying while seeking to tackle the most explosive issues of the Church and the land.

The CC also addressed itself to the Basis for the crisis:

1. Material Basis: The material basis for the crisis could be found in the backward and underdeveloped nature of our society and the consequent existence of a large petty bourgeois influence in our society. This predominant petty bourgeois composition of the society as a whole reflected in the practical work of the CC.
2. The Political and Ideological Basis: As seen in the failure of the CC to study for close to one year which has weakened the extent to which the ideology of Marxism-Leninism acts as a guide to the actions of the members of the higher organs. This failure to study is definitely linked to the non-Leninist manner of functioning, slackness, timidity and "ducking" from making principled criticisms.
3. The Organisational Basis: Seen in the poor functioning of many Party structures, the non-Leninist practices of comrades of higher organs, the inadquate functioning of other Party members in work committees, the lack of reporting, and the objectively based— inability of the O.C. to deal with all matters of discipline further feeds and allows petty bourgeois tendencies to dominate the life of the higher organs of the Party

CROSSROADS
The CC concluded that the Party stood at the crossroads:-

i   The first route would be the petty bourgeois route which would seek to make B's resignation the issue. This would only lead to temporary relief, but would surely lead to the deterioration of the Party into a social-democratic Party and hence the degeneration of the Revolution. This road would be an easy one to follow given the objectively based backwardness and petty bourgeois nature of the society.

ii The second route is the Communist route—the road of Leninist standards and functioning, the road of democratic centralism, of selectivity, of criticism and self-criticism and of collective leadership. The Central Committee reaffirmed the position taken by the General Meeting of September 12th and 13th, 1982— the Party must be placed on a firm Leninist footing.

Political Bureau Meeting
12 October 1983

Report on the meeting of PB [Political Bureau] and CC [Central Committee] held on Oct. 12th given by Cde. Strachan.

—agenda given

—The PB of CC was very concerned about the situation in the Party. He referred to the CC decision on JL [Joint Leadership] and the basis for this. However, following this Cde. MB [Maurice Bishop] felt that he would not give a decision on the CC decision and wanted time to reflect. We were concerned whether DC [Democratic Centralism] would continue to exist. The CC brought the issue to the MS [Members] which lasted 15 hrs. The meeting was the healthiest meeting in history of party (applause). The cdes. stood up for Principles—the unanimity on the resolution. After when MB reached Hungary there was a change. A meeting was held in Hungary [illeg.]. . . . GL [George Louison] gave a Pb opp. [petit-bourgeois opportunist] report and. . . . played a key role in poisoning the mind of MB and manipulating him not to implement the decision. The conduct of GL was totally unbecoming, it was a vulgar behavior, he was caught lying to the PB and CC. The CC immediately expelled GL (applause and chants). We are in a difficult period. We struggled against one [illeg.] for 28 years [Eric Gairy] and would not allow this in our party (applause). . . .How can a leader allow himself to be manipulated by another Cde. GL said he would appeal to M [masses], obviously the M. would have to decide.

Ian Lambert

A bloodshed could have taken place last night it was the rumours that caused this. They said that the country can have only one PM [Prime Minister] because B [Bernard Coard] is a communist. They said they all come from OREL and [illeg.] by B. to take over power. If there is bloodshed it is MB responsibility. Fr. Martin organized a service. MB

---

*Selwyn Strachan had been Minister of Communications, Works and Labour in Bishop's government. He was on Coard's side in the 1983 coup.

has always pointed out where we must stand in class struggle. MB has always said action that is key.

Time and practice would reveal all shades VI [Vladimir Ilyich Lenin] said. Were you ever willing to implement the principle? GL right wing opp. F. Bain has shown emotionalism. The struggle for ideas must be in the party. Who was responsible for the putting the rumour on the street? Come out and talk the truth.

[illeg. name]—

The CC analysed that the party was in tension as a result of the minority. The reason for the rumour. The sit. requires decisiveness. The party is not split. He is disappointed in the content and intent of some cdes. F. Bain has shown little belly, no principles and has behaved as an unruly peasant. Ideo. backwardness of the peasantry. He never addressed the principal issue. He threatened to mobilize agric. workers. He can't speak of resigning. He is like Gairy and this is obj. counter. What he is asking for is a jail. His behavior is against the SC [working class]. The agric. workers must know..On MB—he would have to be expelled from the party. It won't be easy to explain to the masses. We have allowed cultism cult of personality. [illeg. sentence.]

· ·

Peter David

· ·

He spoke about F. Bain on marching workers against the party. He called it Gairy attitude (applause). Many cdes. said that yes that we are moving. Imperialism is watching.

Chris Stroude

We have dealt with this issue too many times and we must take decisions. All who on the CC that are wavering should be removed. F. Bain should be removed from CC. He spoke about honesty and love for masses and GL does not have this. He shocked about MB. He spoke of his pledge, his vacillation. He spoke about the PRAF branch meeting.

The PRAF [People's Revolutionary Armed Forces] would not use guns against the party and revo. The period has steeled us in the PRAF, it has been practical experience. It is not only officers and NCO but everyone. The PRAF wants to see socialism (applause).

Headache

In MB speech he said 3 times he fully accept the blame that JL has not been implemented. He never accepted the decision or changed his mind overseas and he has to come with a cover in order to sell his lines to the party. MB should not be surprised when no one checked him. He spoke of the lack of phone communications. GL phone call to Nelson.

A small clique yet very influential and powerful refusing the CC decision. He called Selwyn brave and courageous.

He spoke of the class character of the whole issue. These elements chose to spread the Afghan line because it is a well known anti-C[ommunist] and anti-Soviet position.

He spoke of key opinion makers. MB is personally responsible for spreading the rumour as a pre-condition for murdering CC and chasing the party of the street. He spoke about Donald told HA. This shows that bourg. know where MB is coming from. They see him as the chosen one to defend the [line missing]. GL is jumping off at the first step on the road to Soc. [Socialism]. He is very disappointed in MB.

Andre McSween [McQueen?]

He said that MB said he never had problems with JL because of he and Uni[son Whiteman]. But now he has to reflect. MB said that the members should not get the minutes but now he brought in to masses. MB knows about the level of the masses and this tried to mobilise the masses. He proposed that the strong supporters should be checked. Proposed that F. Bain should be expelled tonight. Now he has no confidence in GL. Because of B. resignation the CC has made a qalitative leap forward. When our party gets out of this crisis it would be a CP [Communist Party] (applause).

GL

Its a historic discussion. On JL he took an open position. He always taken an open position. His position has always been WC, in interest of build ML [Marxist/Leninist] party. He explained what happened at CC meeting.

. . . .

He said he didn't engage in anything to turn cdes. against the CC. The Cdes. in CC said that it is what he didn't say. There seem to be a report that he and MB was sitting together and discussing strategy and tactics. This is false.

. . . .

Errol George

. . .In Hungary MB was in a low mood. GL, Uni, and MB was in a low mood. GL, Uni, and MB were meeting often when he left for Gda. MB mood was higher. He felt GL was guiding MB. . .

He told MB about rumours of bloodshed. Debourg told him there was an Afghanistan line. . . .

Yvette Joseph

The CC list for confinement is incomplete. GL should be detained. Jackie [Creft] is moving all over the place.

Timoty

Today he met Fitzy who said that CC is lying on MB.

. . . .

Gordon Rachan [Raeburn?]

. . .Can we allow one man to hold up the party? (No) Can we allow a minority to hold the party in ransom? (No) this has led to tension in the party but also tension in the country. He said that the issue must not be taken to the masses but the rt. opp. did so and GL was the main person for doing this.

While there has been a temporary commitment but because of the deep commitment of party cdes. This struggle is turning out to be more and more commitment (applause and ovation). In the coming days we would not be talking about whether you are a party member or not, we will be talking about whether you are a communist or not (applause). The rumour ha smade the work more difficult but we have to tell the workers the truth (applause) who want to go to the masses can go they maybe there for awhile but when the Leninists go the masses they would be there for ever (applause). . . .We have been hiding for years under Gairy now we have to do so under the Pb rt. opp. But we are hiding no longer we will fight out there (applause). Because of the crisis the CC has decided to inform 2 fraternal party—CPSU CC (applause) and PCC CC [Cuban Communist Party] (applause). He called on cdes to be sober in their deliberations and to come up with ideas.

Long Live NJM, Leninism etc.!

8. DEVOURING THE CHILDREN

It is a historian's cliché, but a true one, that revolutions devour their children. Stalin's great terror illustrated the proposition on a horrendous scale. In the microcosm of Grenada, the NJM revolution, too, devoured its children.

People's Army Resolution
12 October 1983

In its opening paragraph the Resolution refers to an Extraordinary General Meeting of the NJM Committee in mid-September 1983 (not reproduced in this collection). At that meeting, Maurice Bishop came under strong criticism, some of it direct, most of it indirect through references to 'dissatisfaction' among the people and charges that, for instance, 'the state of the party at present is the lowest it has been'. One of the members who joined in these attacks was Phyllis Coard, wife of Bernard Coard, leader of the anti-Bishop coup then under preparation.

RESOLUTION OF THE PEOPLE'S REVOLUTIONARY ARMED FORCES BRANCH OF THE NEW JEWEL MOVEMENT

We, the members of the People's Revolutionary Armed Forces Branch of the New Movement gathered this day 12th October 1983 unswervingly support the analysis and ecisions of the New JEWEL Movement Central Committee at its Extraordinary Plenary meeting of September 14th - 17th 1983.

149

We share with deep concern the analysis of the Central Committee on the deep seated crisis and danger which exist in our country and party and therefore wholeheartedly stand by the Central Committee decision to officially establish Joint Leadership in our Party as the correct scientific mode of leadership of our Party, as a decisive step in pulling our Party and Revolution out of its present danger. This decision of the Central Committee was unanimously accepted by all members and candidates of our Party. However, a few opportunist elements in our party are now unashamedly spreading vicious lying rumours to obstruct the implementation of the Central Committee decision.

We recognise and uphold that based on the fundamental Leninist principle of democratic centralism that decision of our Party's Central Committee have the force of law and form the basis of the activity and conduct of all party bodies and of every single party member, candidate member and applicant regardless of their services and posts. We further unswervingly hold high the principles of criticism and self-criticism and collective leadership in our Party as the firm guarantee that our Party will always stay in the correct course and exercise correct leadership and guidance of our Revolution as we struggle to build socialism. Never would we allow cultism, egoism, the unreasonable and unprincipled desires of one man or a minority to be imposed on our Party thus stifling inner party democracy and endangering the party and revolution and holding our country to ransom. We demand an immediate end to this and the restoration of Leninist norms of party life and their strict observance by all as the key for the normal functioning of the party.

We, the members of the People's Revolutionary Armed Forces Branch of the NJM. Uphold as the only reasonable basis for party unity the truth spoken by Comrade Lenin when he said, "Discussing the problem, expressing and hearing different opinions, ascertaining the views of the majority of the organised Marxists, expressing these views in the form of decisions adopted by delegates and carrying them out conscientiously, this is what reasonable people all over the world call unity."

We clearly understand that party discipline is nothing less than the active struggle for the implementation of collectively adopted decisions, such as the decision of the Central committee on Joint

Leadership which was ratified by our entire membership. Therefore, we call on the Central Committee and the entire party to expel from the Party's ranks all elements who do not submit to, uphold and implement in practice the decision of the Central committee and party membership but are bent on holding up the party's work and spreading anti-party propaganda.

The People's Revolutionary Armed Forces Branch of NJM awaits the decision and orders of the Central committee!

LONG LIVE THE NJM CENTRAL COMMITTEE—the highest body and authority of our Party and Revolution!
LONG LIVE THE PARTY—NJM!
LONG LIVE LENINISM!
LONG LIVE OUR PEOPLE'S REVOLUTION!
FORWARD EVER   BACKWARD NEVER!

Castro to Central Committee
15 October 1983

In this letter Fidel Castro indignantly rejects charges by unnamed Grenadian leaders that he and his Cuban Communist Party were 'meddling... in the internal affairs of your Party'. It could be argued, however, that his letter with its explicit support for Bishop, in itself constituted 'meddling'.

EMBASSY OF THE REPUBLIC OF CUBA
GRENADA

The Central Committee
New Jewel Movement
St. George's

Esteemed Comrades:

I send you this message motivated by certain references which, in their conversations with our Ambassador, have been made by several Grenadian leaders in relation to Cuba.

The supposed notion that on passing through our country Bishop had informed me of the problems inside the Party is a miserable piece of slander. Bishop did not mention a single word to me, nor did he make the slightest allusion to the matter. Completely the opposite. He expressed to me in general terms and with great modesty that there were deficiencies in his work which he thought he would overcome in the next few months.

In reality, I am grateful to Bishop for that discretion, and for the respect he showed to his Party and to Cuba by not touching on such matters.

We are indignant at the very thought that some of you would have considered us capable of meddling in any way in the internal questions of your Party. We are people of principle, not vulgar schemers or adventurers.

Everything which happened was for us a surprise, and disagreeable. In our country, the Grenadian Revolution and Comrade Bishop as its central figure were the object of great sympathies and respect. Even explaining the event to our people will not be easy.

In my opinion, the divisions and problems which have emerged will result in considerable damage to the image of the Grenadian Revolution, as much within as outside the country.

Cuba, faithful to its moral values and its international policy, will pay strictest attention to the principle of not interfering in the slightest in the internal affairs of Grenada, fulfilling the promises made in the field of cooperation. Our promises are not to men. They are to the peoples and to principle.

History and developments yet to come will judge what has happened in these last few days.

I wish for you the greatest wisdom, serenity, loyalty to principles, and generosity in this difficult moment through which the Grenadian Revolution is passing.

Cordially,

Commander-in-Chief
Fidel Castro Ruz.   15 October, 1983

Noel to Central Committee
17 October 1983

The writer of this long, rambling letter, Vincent Noel, was a trade union leader. Two days after writing it, he was killed during the Coard coup. The interest of this document lies in its vivid sense of the atmosphere of fear and mutual suspicion that prevailed on the eve of the coup. He had had three talks with Bishop on the latter's return from Hungary. Bishop had complained that only one member of the Central Committee had turned up to meet him at the airport. He professed his readiness to work with Coard and even under him. 'But he said that in recent times he had been become [sic] increasingly convinced, from all the bits and pieces of evidence available to him, that there were behind the scenes, unprincipled manoeuvres to remove him by a section of the CC.' In this conviction, of course, he was not mistaken.

TOP STAFF

                                                              17.10.83

Members of the Central Committee and Party,

There seem to be some confusion as to what transpired on the occasion when I met Maurice last week. I was told by Gemma on Saturday that on enquiring from Owusu she was told that I was being kept at home because no one knew what had been discussed between Maurice and myself on the occasions that we met.

I met and spoke to Maurice three times since he returned from Hungary. Prior to that the only conversations I had with Maurice for months were at the meetings of the workers Committee and sub-committee.

The first time I spoke to Maurice was last Tuesday night at his house from about ten o'clock until sometime after twelve. He telephoned and asked me to come up in response to two unsuccessful calls I had made to him on Monday and Tuesday afternoons.

We spoke first of all about his trip to Eastern Europe and then my trip to Jamaica. We also spoke about the local and regional trade union situation and especially the upcoming C.C.L. Congress. Finally I introduced the discussion of the Party stating that I had picked up from various comrades that he had not accepted the decision of the Party on Joint Leadership.

Maurice denied that he had any problems with Joint Leadership and went into a long history of his acceptance of that principle dating back to the formation of the Movement. He stated that he himself had voted for Joint Leadership at the meeting of full members of the Party, but at that time and at the meeting of the Central Committee he had expressed certain reservations. These reservations were reinforced during his trip and by certain developments since his return.

His first concern was the question of the precise operationalising of Joint Leadership; the second was historical precedent. My response was that 'operationalising' was a detail to be worked out and that ours was a dynamic process which could not be dogmatically patterned after historical precedence. He retorted that it was a tiny detail like a fuse that could cause a car or aeroplane to stall or take off.

The third concern of Maurice was the attitude of comrades of the C.C. to him since his return. He complained that quite unnaturally only one comrade of the entire C.C., Selwyn, was present to meet him at the airport and that Selwyn's greeting had been cold. Further, that no other comrade of the C.C., save H.A., had checked him. Contrary to long established practice neither Owusu nor Headache as chiefs of the Interior and Army respectively had come to give him any report.

I responded to Maurice by suggesting that there may have been a very simple explanation for the number of comrades who met him at the airport. Some comrades may not have been informed or were simply pressed with work. I pointed out that while I was a member of the P.B. I rarely went to the airport either to see him leave or arrive. On the question of comrades of the C.C. checking him I asked Maurice whether HE had tried to establish contact with them. He replied no. I told him that as chairman of the C.C. the ultimate responsibility for establishing contact with members of the C.C. must lay with him. He agreed and said that he was planning to raise that and all his other concerns at a meeting of the P.B. scheduled for the next day, Wednesday 12th.

I queried Maurice as to whether he would raise the fact that only Selwyn met him at the airport as one of his concerns. He said yes. I responded by saying that in my opinion the question of how many people met him at the airport was objectively a pettybourgeois concern and I could not see members of the P.B. treating it in any other way. The comrade replied that that would be correct if it was a single incident standing by itself but it had to be seen within the wider context of all the other things which were happening.

I answered the comrade by saying that if anything was happening other than what I had read in the minutes and been told by party members who were at the general meeting then I did not know. What I did know, I explained, was that several party comrades were accusing him of holding up the work of the party through his non acceptance of Joint Leadership. Some comrades had gone so far as to say that he could not go beyond social democracy. Maurice appeared visibly hurt by that last statement.

After a long pause the comrade responded saying that what was of stake was much more than whether he had petit bourgeois qualities or weaknesses. He said that he had picked up a line which spoke of an "Afghanistan Solution". I was stunned by this. While Maurice was out of the country De Bourg had said to me one day that Chalkie had told him that there would be a solution like Afghanistan if the Chief fucked around on the question of Joint Leadership. At the time that De Bourg told me this I had dismissed Chalkie's remarks as a lot of irresponsible nonsense but Maurice's statement shook me.

I told Maurice that I had heard the Afghan talk before and where I had heard it. He said that in his case he had picked it up as coming from Ram Folkes through one of his personnel security comrade. He did not name the comrade. I said to Maurice that if things had descended to the level of PS. [Personnel Security] men taking sides and talking of Afghanistan then we were a fraction away from bloodshed and disaster. I assured the comrade that the position that I had adopted on Joint Leadership was based purely on principle and my understanding of the issues involved, not personality. I then questioned him about his personal relationship to other comrades within the C.C. as I was of the opinion that he had good relations with all and in particular Selwyn, H.A., Owusu and Bernard.

He claimed that until recently he had excellent relations with all comrades except Bernard with whom he had had strained relations for about one year. He gave an example of the good relations with Owusu, for instance, and spoke of a report that Owusu had written about the U.S. Trip which report embarrassed him (Maurice) because of the hero worship it contained.

As regards Bernard he said that relations had been strained for about one year since his resignation from the C.C. He recounted his years of association with Bernard from school days up to October last year. Her said that when Bernard resigned last year he did his best to get Bernard to withdraw it recognising the many talents of the comrade and his value at the leadership level. But Bernard refused to withdraw the resignation and decided to go to Carriacou instead. During that period he became apprehensive that Bernard was contemplating suicide and for that reason called in Keith Roberts and asked him to follow Bernard to Carriacou and ensure his safety.

Maurice said that as far as he was concerned he could work along with Bernard even if Bernard was chosen outright as leader of the party.

But he said that in recent times he had been become increasingly convinced, from all the bits and pieces of evidence available to him, that there were behind the scenes, unprincipled manoeuvres to remove him by a section of the C.C. I again told the comrade that the position I had taken was based on the minutes I had read, the account of the general meeting and my desire, like all other party comrades, to push the party forward. I urged Maurice to formally appeal the decision on Joint Leadership if he had a problem with it and to also raise all the other issues frankly and openly at the meeting of the P.B. the next morning as the situation was grave and could only get worse.

Maurice repeated that he had no problems with Joint Leadership subject to clarification on operationalisation. But, Maurice went on, the main concern at this time was the behind the scenes manoeuvres against him. I again urged Maurice to raise that openly at the P.B. the next day. He told me not to worry that he would deal with everything. The conversation more or less ended there and I left.

That night (Tuesday) I did not sleep. The more I thought about what Maurice had said the more worried I became. Next morning instead of going to the International Airport as usual I went to H.A.'s house and told him of my grave concern about the situation in the party and in particular the fear of bloodshed. H.A. said that the situation was worse than I thought and that I could not be more concerned than he was.

He said that, for instance, there was a meeting of some comrades in the army that very morning to discuss the situation in the party and he had no idea who precisely had called the meeting as he had not been officially informed. Further, he said that the tension among C.C. members was so high that they had stopped sleeping in their houses. I told H.A. that that was madness and demanded that the P.B. sit down that morning and fully and completely thrash out all the problems and suspicions. He agreed. The conversation between H.A. and I was a very short one. It lasted only for the time it took me to drive from his house to Fort Frederick in my car.

When I left H.A. I went down to Selwyn to again raise my concern. Selwyn agreed with my analysis of the serious state of tension existing within the party but said Maurice was the one to blame because he had refused to accept in practice, Joint Leadership as agreed upon by the entire party. He said that he was hearing about the 'Afghan solution' for the first time, and, that contrary to that, it was Maurice who had been planning to kill members of the C.C. He said that within the past few days a lot of evidence had come to light. For instance, last year St. Paul had approached another security man to kill Bernard after he resigned from the C.C. I retold to Selwyn what Maurice had told me about taking measures to prevent Bernard from committing suicide after his resignation from the C.C. and I commented that it seemed to me that the C.C. was suffering from an overdose of paranoia.

Selwyn said that the only problem at the C.C. was that Maurice would not conform to Democratic Centralism and that he was being encouraged in this by Right Opportunists. He said that Maurice had now compounded the problem by taking the party's business to the Cubans in an unfraternal and unprincipled way using his personal friendship with Fidel. Selwyn claimed that Maurice had spent two extra days in Cuba just for this, and, that as a show of support for Maurice, Fidel had given a reception for Maurice at which eight members of the Political Bureau had been present including Fidel and Raoul. Obviously I could not respond to Selwyn's charges but I became fully and absolutely convinced that the party and Revolution were on the brink of disaster. Later that day Nazim, De Bourg and I were at Nutmeg Restaurant discussing the crisis within the party. Towards the end of the discussion Naz intimated that he, Mikey, and Chess and others had written a joint letter to Maurice asking for an audience to discuss the current crisis. Naz asked me whether I would join the group and if so to check Maurice to set up the time for the meeting since I was already in contact with him. I agreed but said I could not do anything until after 7.00 p.m. since I had a Branch meeting at Grenville from 4.30 p.m. until about 6.00 p.m.

That afternoon I had two shocking experiences. "Ma Lottie" Phillip and then Lyden confronted me with a rumour they had picked up that Bernard and Phyl were trying to depose and kill Maurice. I tried to squash the rumour by denying that anything like that was going on in our party. But I was horrified that our internal problems were among the masses in that way.

I returned to town from my branch meeting at Grenville at about 6.30 p.m. that evening and stopped off at Gemma on my way down. From there I made three unsuccessful calls to Nazim, Maurice and Selwyn. I left Gemma's house and went directly to Maurice's but I was told by "Bulo" that he was still at the meeting at the fort, meaning the P.B./C.C. meeting. From Maurice I went to visit my children at Maria. I was very tired having not slept properly for many nights. I dozed off and eventually stayed there for the night making no contact with anyone.

The next morning (Thursday 13th) I checked Chess on my way home. I told him about the rumours. We analysed that the rumour had not yet hit the working class and decided on a common approach to diffuse it if it did begin to circulate. We recognised the additional grave dangers created by the rumours and agreed that we would, together with Naz etc., check Maurice later than morning after a meeting which he (Chess) had at the power station. I agreed to contact Maurice on my way to the office. This I did.

I arrived at Maurice's house shortly after 8.00 a.m. and remained for about 30 or 40 minutes. He asked me to wait in the conference room while he finished a 'rap' with George Louison in his bedroom. When Maurice came back to the conference room our encounter was very brief. I asked him whether he had received a letter from Naz etc. requesting an audience. He said yes and that he was willing to meet party comrades at any time subject to other pressing engagements. He asked when precisely we wanted the meeting. I replied about 4 or 5 o'clock but that I would get back to him about 1 o'clock. Maurice looked terrible I asked him if he had slept the night before. He answered negatively. I advised him to stop smoking, relax, get some sleep and then I left. I made no mention of the rumour only because I did not want to burden the comrade with further worries just then.

A short while after I got down to the union office Chalkie came in and we greeted each other in the usual way. I asked him how were things going at the level of the C.C. as things were beginning to get rough on the ground. I mentioned the rumours. Chalkie said "What rumours that? Is the chief that start that shit. So you don't know what going on? Come ah go show you."

We went into his office and began to talk. He told me tht Maurice had started the rumour about himself, using Erry George, who had confessed, and St. Paul [illeg.] that Maurice was a psychopath and last year tried to kill Bernard after he resigned. That the night before (Wednesday 12/10/83) Maurice using George Louison had organised Bourgeois elements in St. Paul's (Bulleu, Donald etc.) to take arms from the St. Paul's Militia Camp to go Mt. Walldale to defend Maurice. That George had been removed from the P.B. and C.C.

I told Chalkie that he was mad that I could not believe what I was hearing about Maurice. Chalkie replied that it was Maurice who was power crazy. After that conversation with Chalkie I must have looked visibly shaken as both Frog (union officer) and my secretary asked me if something was wrong. I asked my secretary to cancel all appointments for the day. I then tried to get both Chess and Naz neither of whom was in office.

As I left the union office I saw Carl Johnson and others in front of the Party Secretariat. I went there and asked C.J. for Chess. He said that Chess was still at the Power Station. There were all sort of excited bilateral taking place among party comrades at the secretariat. I left there and went directly back to Maurice's house. He was alone and I was told by the security to go into his bedroom.

I told Maurice about the rumour and related to him what Chalkie had said. He confirmed the unpleasant development but denied having anything to do with the origin of the rumour and organisation of armed vigilante. Maurice gave me a blood chilling account of what had happened at the C.C. meeting the day before. He said that members of the C.C., particularly Chalkie, kept pulling out their weapons threateningly during the whole meeting and that Fitzy had freaked out partly as a result of that. I told Maurice that what was going on was madness, that the membership had a right to know and that he should lay everything bare before the membership in the general meeting planned for that afternoon. He asked me what general meeting I was talking about. I explained that Chalkie [illeg.] told me that there was a meeting of all ranks of the party, from applicants up, to explain the present situation within the party.

Maurice explained that he had been at a meeting of the Central Committee until late the night before and that no such general meeting had been proposed or agreed. He offered it as another example of the plotting against him and said he would not go. I pleaded with Maurice to attend the meeting as any other action may be interpreted by the membership as an admission of guilt. Maurice complained of not feeling well and said he really did not know whether he could stand the emotional strain of a meeting such as the last general meeting.

Eventually I got Maurice to agree for me to get a doctor, namely Bernard Gittens, to attend to him. At the same time, while I went for the doctor he was supposed to start putting his notes together for the meeting that afternoon so that even if he was given sedation by the doctor he would still be prepared at the meeting. As I left to go for the doctor I was worried not only about the state of the party and Maurice's physical health but the possibility of his committing suicide also crossed my mind.

As I was about to enter my car and leave I was approached by one of the Personnel Security men and told that I was under arrest. I was taken to under the mango tree in Bernard's yard and interviewed by Chalkie and Ian St. Bernard. I was told by the two comrades that the Central Committee had decided that I should be arrested for conspiring with Maurice. They could not answer conspiring about what and refused to say if Maurice was still a member of the C.C. In brief I explained to the comrades that I had not been involved in anything resembling conspiracy and was only going to get a doctor for Maurice. I asked him (St. B.) to send to get Dr. Gittens for Maurice while he clarified matters. He told me not to worry that a strong "delegation" would go to visit Maurice in a short while. I was then taken to my house and ordered to stay there or be formally detained. All arms and ammunition which I have always carried were taken away.

About 3.45 p.m. that afternoon I received a note through Chess from Ian St. Bernard authorising me to attend the general meeting of the party. Given the extremely serious nature of what we were there to discuss, one would have thought that the discussions and decisions would have taken place in a calm and sober way. Instead led by members of the Political Bureau, the meeting was a horrendous display of militarism, hatred and emotional vilification. Never before have I witnessed this trend within our party and on no grounds can this conduct be justified.

This trend has continued in public and on the public media. A horrible lie is being spread that 'Brat' Bullen and the other persons who went to the St. Paul's militia camp to collect arms did so to go and kill Bernard and Phyl. This is a lie known to the whole party. What was said by Chalkie to me on the morning of Thursday 13th and repeated at the general meeting by both H.A. and Owusu was that they had gone to get arms to go and protect 'their Chief' because he was in danger. Let me make it very clear, however that I disagree fundamentally with the action taken by that group and support the measures taken by the security forces.

In my over 10 years of association with our party never one day have I had reason to despair, not even when I was removed from the Political Bureau in 1981. For 20 years I have dreamt of building a socialist and communist society. We began our march forward with our Glorious Revolution but, today, by our own collective irresponsibility we have begun to cannabilise ourselves.

The crime that we are committing is not only against our Party, People and Revolution. Our crime is against the entire world revolutionary process and the Caribbean masses in particular.

You know no less than I that our Revolution is not irreversible. And while we brutally destroy ourselves, the corbeau [crow] of imperialism and reaction anxiously make preparation to pounce.

For the past four or five days I have stayed at home following the threats of Chalkie and Ian St. Bernard. Several comrades have checked me to find out what happened and my position on various things. I have made it clear that from the time I read the minutes and obtained some specific clarity on a few issues I accepted the decision on Joint Leadership. But even if I did not that is my right as a party member so long as I did not seek to subvert in anyway the Democratic Centralist decision of the party. Or have we now new norms?

For the past four or five days I have allowed myself to be confined as a counter-revolutionary criminal. Perhaps a conscious attempt is being made to push me into adventurous objectively counter-revolutionary activity so that I can be discredited afterwards. But that will never happen!

If I am to be sacrificed to suit the expediency of any person or persons then it is my duty as a communist to prevent it if I can. When I chose the road to revolution above all else including family I knew that I could be martyred at any time. But frankly, comrades, at no time did I vaguely dream that that threat would come from within our own party. My only crime is that I spoke to Maurice Bishop, chairman of our Central Committee and Prime Minister, in a principled way about the same things that all other comrades in the party were discussing in a million bilaterals.

I request that my letter be discussed by the C.C. and be circulated to all members of the party in the same way that the Resolution from the Armed Forces was circulated last Thursday 13th October.

Long live inner party democracy!

Long live our Party!

Long live Socialsm and Communism!

Fraternally

[signature]

Vince

Main Political Department Bulletin
20 October 1983

This document records events of the previous day, in Leninist language and obvious selectivity. The 'masses of the people' were said to have broken into the home of Maurice Bishop. With Unison White-

man and Vincent Noel, Bishop had begun 'arming people who rep-
resented their own minority class interest'. But 'because of the prompt
action of the reserve force, guided by the Central Committee of the
NJM, these betrayers of the masses were crushed'. Had Bishop won,
he and his supporters would doubtless have made an identical
claim.

BULLETIN FROM THE MAIN POLITICAL DEPARTMENT
20/10/83
THEIR HEROISM IS AN EXAMPLE FOR US

Comrade soldiers, yesterday 19th October, the masses of people led by
Unison Whiteman broke into the home of Maurice Bishop in defiance
to warning shots fired in the air by the soldiers of People's
Revolutionary Armed Forces. They then took Maurice Bishop into the
streets of St. George's. They wanted to hear Maurice Bishop speak.
Maurice Bishop, Unison Whiteman, Vincent Noel, Fitzroy Bain,
Jacquelin Creft and other people of the bourgeois and upper petty
bourgeois strata, known counter-revolutionaries and Gairyites led the
crowd onto Port Rupert, the Headquarters of the People's
Revolutionary Armed Forces where they forced through the main
entrance, beating the Comrade Sister who was trying to prevent them
from entering and over-running the Army Headquarters and disarming
the Officers and Soldiers. Einstein Louison, former chief of the
General Staff who had been suspended was called by Maurice and proclaimed Commander-in-Chief and Chief of Staff to the People's
Revolutionary Armed Forces. Einstein Louison then proceeded to
issue arms and ammunition to the people. It must be noted that when
Einstein Louison started distributing the weapons, Vincent Noel asked
who were the trained militia in the crowd for them to step forward
because there were some men that had 'to be passed out'. Soldiers on
Port Rupert took off their clothes and said that they could not take part
in such an Army. Important to note that some of the comrade sister
Soldiers were beaten and stripped by Maurice Bishop, Vincent Noel,
Fitzroy Bain and their petty bourgeois and bourgeois supporters. One
heroic sister, Pte. Racheal Abraham then went up to Maurice Bishop

and in his face told him that he was responsible for all that had happened.

It is very important to note that when the masses of people called on Maurice Bishop to speak they were told by Vincent Noel that Maurice Bishop could not speak to them because he was in a very important meeting. Comrades, the masses had no intention to cause bloodshed but in their confusion they were led by Maurice Bishop and his petty bourgeois and bourgeois friends as cannon fodder to cause bloodshed. Comrades, it is very important to recognise the heroism of our People's Revolutionary Armed Forces. When WO2 Rapheal Mason and Sargeant Byron Cameron were shot one sister Pte. Patricia Frank tore up her jersey to bandage the chest and leg of those wounded comrades. She then went clad in pants and bra to mobilise a fire truck to put out the flames at Port Rupert. She was prevented from doing this and she later went to get nurses to evacuate a sister who in her fright had jumped over the wall at Port Rupert and was seriously injured. She also went to the hospital to explain to the people there than counter-revolutionaries had opened fire on our soldiers. This is an example of true love and heroism, the qualities that we must develop further.

Pte. Lynessa Frederick stood firmly with weapon in hand preventing the crowd of people from going up to the Armoury to get arms until she was overpowered by them and her weapon taken.

Corporal Nerril Richards greatly assisted in boosting the morale of the comrades there and inspiring them with his staunchness to stand firm.

Comrade Lance Corporal Godfrey Thomas advancing with WO2 Rapheal Mason to give covering fire to OC Mayers in the counter attack was told by comrade Mason that he comrade Mason had been shot. On reaching comrade Mason, Lance Corporal Thomas was pushed by WO2 Mason who told him to continue the advance. Comrade Thomas refused to go on without assisting comrade Mason. While holding comrade Mason, comrade Thomas said he saw a man suddenly rise up from behind a wall with a weapon and he heard a bullet strike the BTR and penetrate comrade Thomas's pants. Comrade Mason then said that he had again been shot and told comrade Thomas that he could not make it and that he should be taken to the hospital. On the way to the hospital, comrade Mason collapsed and told comrade Thomas to take care of his son because he was going to die. Comrade Mason was taken by some civilians to the hospital where he later died. Comrade Thomas then pushed back to meet the BTR and on his way up saw Lance Corporal Martin Simon with his chest streaming blood. Even in that condition comrade Simon warned comrade Thomas that the masses were shooting at them and that he should be careful. While at the same time assisted OC Mayers, who was also shot. Comrade Thomas left comrade Simon in the care of some civilians who took him to hospital. OC Conrad Mayers led the first squad into the attack shouting "For the Defence of the Homeland". He was clearing his way to move further on up the Port when he was shot by a man shooting directly.

REVOLUTIONARY SOLDIERS AND MEN OF THE PEOPLE'S REVOLUTIONARY ARMED FORCES

Today our People's Revolutionary Army has gained victory over the right opportunist and reactionary forces which attacked the Head-quarters of our Ministry of Defence. These anti-worker elements using the working people as a shield entered Port Rupert.

Our patriotic men, loving the masses and rather than killing them since we understood that they were being used, we held our fire. However, the leadership of the counter-revolutionary elements, led by Maurice Bishop, Unison Whiteman and Vincent Noel, knowing that we did not want to harm the people disarmed the Officers and Chiefs and soldiers and began arming people who represented their own minority class interest.

Comrades, these men who preached for us that they had the interest of the Grenadian people at heart did not have one member of the work-ing class controlling their criminal operations. These elements although they used the working class and working people to gain their objective did not have any confidence in them and therefore had only businessmen, nuns, nurses and lumpen elements in the operations centre.

The presence of the people shows as clearly where they are coming from. Besides, Maurice Bishop certain that they had won, pointed out to the Officers that he did not want to have socialism built in this country.

These counter-revolutionaries who had given the assurance in the Party before to resolve the crisis peacefully—were on the one hand trying to give assurance to the unarmed soldiers that nothing would happen while on the other hand they were preparing to murder all Party comrades, Officers and Chiefs that they held. Again this truth was borne out when Maurice Bishop openly stated that he was going to build a new Party and a new Army—to defend the interest of the bourgeois.

However, because of the prompt action of the reserve force, guided by the Central Committee of the N.J.M.—these betrayers of the masses were crushed. The timely move of our Motorized Units dealt a devastating blow to these criminals, those opportunist elements who did not want to see socialism built in our country and who were not interested in seeing the masses benefit more and more.

Comrades, today Wednesday 19th October, history was made again. All patriots and revolutionaries will never forget this day when counter-revolution, the friends of imperialism were crushed. This victory today will ensure that our glorious Party the N.J.M. will live on and grow from strength to strength leading and guiding the Armed Forces and the Revolution.

This victory is ongoing progress and for socialism. But in giving this victory, one of our soliders. Sgt. Byron Cameron was wounded, while O. Cdt Conrad Mayers, WO2 Raphael Mason, Sgt. Darrel Peters and L. Cpl. Martin Simon died a heroes death.

Let our comrades death be an inspiration to us, let it be a sign of the staunchness of our revolutionary Armed Forces and let us use it to strengthen our resolve to defend the Revolution and to build socialism.

Let this moment be proof to counter-revolution of our firmness, discipline and staunchness to the Party, the N.J.M., the working class, working people and to socialism. Let this be testimony of our unity behind our Party and Revolution.

We have won a victory comrades, but let us stand and be united to ensure that we achieve other victories.

LONG LIVE OUR PARTY, THE N.J.M.!!
LONG LIVE THE PEOPLE'S REVOLUTIONARY ARMED FORCES!!
LONG LIVE THE GRENADA REVOLUTION!!
FORWARD EVER!!   BACKWARD NEVER!!!

SOCIALISM OR DEATH!!!

9. THE SOCIALIST INTERNATIONAL CONNECTION

The Socialist International was founded at a special congress in Frankfurt in 1951 and is based in London. In effect, it was a re-creation of the Second International, itself a revival of the original First International or International Workers' Association founded in London in 1864. It should of course be sharply distinguished from the Third International (Lenin's Comintern) and from the Fourth (Trotskyist). For many years, the SI stood in the front rank in the battle against communism. In the 1970s, however, many of the Socialist and Social Democratic member parties of the SI were increasingly penetrated by communists, in line with the resolutions of the Karlovy Vary (Carlsbad) conference of communist parties in 1967. Under the Chairmanship of Chancellor (now ex-Chancellor) Willy Brandt, and under two strong left-wing influences—Egon Bahr of the West German Social Democratic Party (SPD) and the late Olof Palme, the Swedish Prime Minister—the SI strongly favoured continuing contacts with the Soviet Union, through the International Department of the CPSU's Central Committee (the real successor of the Comintern). The important documents in this section demonstrate the extent of Soviet subversion and penetration of the SI.

Panama Meeting of SI
3 March 1981

The situation in El Salvador was the sole item on the agenda of this 'emergency meeting'. The Report, prepared for the NJM leadership, records the fact that General Vernon Walters, a former deputy Director of the American Central Intelligence Agency (CIA), was denied a hearing when he wished to provide proof of Cuban and Soviet arms

169

*supplies to the rebel guerrillas. The Salvadoran MNR (Movimiento
Nacional Revolucionario), represented at the meeting by Héctor
Oqueli, claimed social democratic credentials, but served as a propa-
ganda front for the Marxist–Leninists. It was run by Dr Guillermo
Manuel Ungo who was also a leader of the political front, the FDR or
Frente Democrático Revolucionaria. He is indeed the only leader of
the FDR not to have been involved in violence. At the time of the
meeting, the guerrillas in El Salvador were communist-controlled
and were in receipt of arms and other aid from the Soviet Union, East
Germany, North Vietnam, Cuba and Nicaragua.*

*The Report mentions an apparently unsuccessful attempt by Carlos
Andrés Pérez, a former President of Venezuela and leader of that
country's Acción Democrática party to add the names of Cuba and the
Soviet Union to a resolution calling for an end to the supply of arms to
El Salvador. The Swedish Social Democratic Party was represented
by Brent Carlsson and the Jamaican PNP (People's National Party),
by Michael Manley, who was Prime Minister of Jamaica until
1980.*

TO: N.J.M. Leadership
FROM: Comrade Whiteman
SUBJECT: Emergency S.I. Meeting in Panama
DATE: March 3, 1981

The emergency S.I. meeting of Latin America and the Caribbean took
place in Panama on Saturday, 28th February and Sunday, 1st March.
Basically, it was a one item agenda; the situation in El Salvador.

There were representatives of the following countries:

Argentina, Barbados, Bolivia, Chile, Costa Rica, El Salvador,
Ecuador, Guatemala, Grenada, Honduras, Panama itself, Peru,
Puerto Rico, Dominican Republic, Venezuela, Uraguay and
Nicaragua. P.N.P. was absent. From Europe came Spain, West
Germany, France, Portugal and Sweden arrived. Brent Carlsson,
Secretary General attended. Media coverage was wide.

The Conference was designed to counter these two carefully worked
out tactics by the United States:

(1) To project the struggle of the people of El Salvador as a direct East West ("Communist - Capitalist") confrontation as a means of completely wiping out from the consciousness of the world the domestic causes, the oligarchy, the semi-feudal system, the incredible poverty of the masses.

(2) To show that the freedom fighters ("Marxist hardliners") do not want a negotiated settlement, that they prefer the bloodshed.

Because of airline difficulties, I missed the first day of the Conference. Although S.I. has a clear concensus on El Salvador, somehow Carlos Andre Perez insisted on adding the names of Cuba and the Soviet Union to the resolution demanding an end to the supply of arm to El Salvador! (He claims that he is not anti-Cuba or anti-Communist but that S.I. must appear to be objective and even handed. He also claims that he whole heartedly supports the El Salvador liberation struggle. This is strange because there was a quiet meeting where the military commanders in the field explained their need for support in this critical situation and Carlos agreed with them).

For hours he persisted. Sweden and Grenada spoke out forcefully on the issue. Grenada pointed out that the U.S. supply of arms to the junta is a notorious fact, that the U.S. officially and publicly stated this; that S.I. should not speculate on where the freedom fighters are getting arms from; that, in any event, we should not equate arms for the oppressors with weapons to defend the people in their just struggle.

Finally, the El Salvador Comrades said they were prepared to accept a compromise formula that names no country but makes it clear that it is the U.S. that is being condemned. The house accepted this approach.

It should be noted that Vernon Walters, the ex-deputy C.I.A. Director insisted on presenting to the meeting (he is on a tour of the region to drum up support for a U.S. invasion of El Salvador and he happened to be in Panama by "coincidence") proof of Cuban and Soviet arms supplies. This offer was not accepted.

As a means of defeating the second U.S. tactics ("hardliners, not wanting to negotiate"), the Conference offered the services of S.I. Chairman, Willy Brandt as mediator in the conflict.

This initiative ensures that the U.S. cannot propose someone favourable to their own interest. Brandt is sympathetic for the freedom fighters but the U.S. will have difficulty rejecting him for he is a Nobel Peace Prize Winner with stature world wide.

This counter tactic would therefore give the comrades time to carry on the military and the political struggle together.

Another resolution expressed support for the Nicaraguan and Grenada revolutionary processes and solidarity with the Government and people of Panama who were undergoing pressures from the U.S. There was also support for Michael Manley and for the independence of Puerto Rico.

A Working Group for Latin America and the Caribbean was chosen. The members are Jose Pena Gomez, Carlos Andres Perez, Hector Oqueli, Bernt Carlsson, N.J.M. and P.N.P. This group will propose to S.I. structures and a work programme for the region.

For a number of reasons, I proposed a regional conference in Grenada in May. The conference enthusiastically accepted. Delegates from all over expressed interest in coming to Grenada to the meeting and this will be extremely useful to us also. If the N.J.M. Bureau ratifies this, plans for the conference will have to begin soon after the Festival.

The General Secretary, Bernt Calsson, will be visiting us for a few days on April 18, and Pierre Schori sometime in May. These are also two important visits for us since they are stalwart supporters of the revolution in S.I. and internationally.

. . . .

Many of the leading comrades will be at the Aruba meeting. They look forward to seeing comrade Maurice.

The next two major S.I. (International) events are the Party Leaders' Conference - Amsterdam - April 29, and the Bureau meeting - Tel Aviv on June 11, and 12. I strongly recomend that Comrade Maurice attend one of these.

P.S. On my way back from the Conference I noted the following from press reports:

(1) That the mission of Vernon Walters to the region has been considered a failure. Of course, he claims that his objective was not to gain support for a U.S. invasion of El Salvador but merely to explain and give evidence of Cuban and Soviet military involvement.

(2) That the big four Latin American powers: Argentina, Brazil, Venezuela and Mexico have issued a statement in Buenos Aires rejecting any U.S. intervention in El Salvador.

(3) That Duarte has agreed to participate in the mediation talks as proposed by Socialist International.

(4) That Bernt Carlsson is on his way to Washington to discuss the mediation offer with the State Department.

(5) That the U.S. has just announced a massive step up of military aid to El Salvador. (Many U.S. Senators, even Senator John Glenn who once supported such a policy are now opposed to this).

(6) It seems that both sides are applying the tactic of talk more, appear the one more willing to talk, but fight harder.

SI Presidium Meeting in Bonn
1 April 1982

Once again, Central America dominated this Socialist International meeting. The role of the Grenadian delegates as agents for the Soviet Union and Cuba in pressing for support for the Sandinista government in Nicaragua and for the guerrillas in El Salvador is quite clear. The Chilean delegation consisted of representatives not of the late President Salvador Allende's Socialist Party but of the Radical Party, a centrist group which, however, supported Allende's election in 1970, thereby losing many of its more conservative members.

To: Cde. Unison Whiteman, Foreign Minister
From: Cde. Fennis Augustine, High Commissioner

Report on Meeting of the Praesidium of Socialist International held in Bonn, West Germany on 1–2 April 1982

I arrived at the Tulpenfeld Hotel, Bonn where most of the delegates were staying at about 4.00 p.m. Unfortunately, I was unable to obtain accommodation at that hotel. Arrangements were subsequently made for me at Astoria Hotel, a reasonable distance away from Tulpenfeld.

After settling in, I returned to Tulpenfeld. There was a meeting with the Cuban delegation, the Nicaraguan delegation, the British delegation which was headed by Michael Foot, leader of the Labour Party, the Guatamalan delegation, the Venezuelan delegation headed by Carlos Cuidros [Andres] Perez, a member of the Swedish delegation and Guillermo Lingo [Ungo] of the El Salvador delegation.

Before these meetings I spoke to representatives and later on Bernt Carlsson Secretary General of the Socialist International seeking observer status for Grenada at the meeting. The decision was firm that only members of the Praesidium and specially invited guest could attend. (The composition of the Praesidium is; President, General Secretary, six Honorary Presidents, and twenty-one Vice Presidents).

ISSUES:

The special meeting of the Praesidium was called because of the confusion existing in S.I. over a number of issues, one delegate said to me that if nothing is done about the present situation S.I. would lose credibility.

(a) The most immediate was the cancellation of the Bureau meeting which was to take place in Venezuela, when the Party Democratic Action bowed to American pressure and refused to invite Nicaragua. It was cancelled on the personal intervention of Bernt Carlsson and Willy Brandt.

(B) The declaration by Nicaragua of a state of emergency, seen in

the context of the debate taking place within S.I. as to the principles involved in Social Democracy i.e. elections, two party system, human rights question, freedom of religion, freedom of
speech (free press).

(c) Disarmament—The recent visit of the S.I. disarmament committee to the Soviet Union within the context of world
disarmament.

(The East—West conflict as it is seen being aggravated by
Poland, Afghanistan and the debate about the relationship
with Cuba.

The meeting started at 09.45 on the 1st April, although a number of
delegations had not yet arrived. Some of the late arrivals were, French
delegation, Israeli delegation, Austrian delegation, Jamaican delegation (only Michael Manley attended Cde. Paul Miller did not attend),
Danish delegation and the Netherland delegation and the Chilean
delegation Radical Party (Cde. Anselmo Sule was the only delegate
attending).

Central America and the Caribbean was down for discussion in the
afternoon session (see agenda attached) it generated the most
interest.

My information is that the discussion on Central America and the
Caribbean went very well, this is subtantiated by the fact that:-

(a) There appear to be some dissatisfaction with Felipe Gonzales's
report on Nicaragua—one delegate referred to the report as
somewhat vague.

(b) A committee was appointed to draft resolution on the area
(resolution attached) the composition of the committee was Ed
Broadbent, Canada; Carlos Perez, Venezuelan; Michael
Manley, Jamaica; and later on Gunselmo Sule was coopted.

(c) A decision was taken that Willy Brandt should appoint a committee to visit the area and report back (I asked Brent Carlsson
that Grenada be included in the itinerary of the committee).

(d) It was decided that the S.I. Secretariat will continue to invite
Nicaragua to attend its meeting, implication being disapproval

with Democratic Action of Venezuela over its decision to exclude Nicaragua from the Bureau meeting in November.

I had a short discussion with Michael Manley—his stay was extremely short—he advised that based on the letter he received from Maurice, Grenada's case was put firmly by him. My understanding is that this was so, although there appear to be some confusion on the invitation. In a follow up discussion, Brent Carlsson informed me that N.J.M. will have to send our individual invitations to Sister Parties.

On the East/West question—it appears that the meeting supported West Germany's position on Ostpolitick and to press for constructive dialogue on disarmament.

Comments

Most sister parties seemed well disposed towards Grenada, although some have reservations on what they see as the Marxist thrust of the N.J.M. I believe that close relationship with Cuba will continue. Nicaragua's position is a little more difficult, although there was a great degree of understanding and sympathy for them by the time the meeting was finished.

Secret Caucus in Managua
6–7 January 1983

One of the most important and revealing documents in the entire collection. The secret regional caucus of the SI was set up on Fidel Castro's orders to give his Communist Party a totally irregular voice in a gathering of ostensibly socialist parties. Some of the organisations taking part have been mentioned in earlier notes, but for the convenience of readers, the following is a full glossary:

FSLN: Frente Sandinista de Liberación Nacional, the ruling party of Nicaragua.

MNR: Movimiento Nacional Revolucionario of El Salvador (the 'respectable' front for the Marxist–Leninist guerrillas).

RP: Radical Party of Chile; not a socialist party but supported the late President Allende, leader of the Socialist Party.

PNP: *People's National Party of Jamaica.*
PCC: *Partido Comunista de Cuba.*
WPA: *Working People's Alliance of Guyana.*
PLP: *Progressive Labour Party of Saint Lucia.*
NDP: *National Democratic Party of Austria.*
FDR: *Frente Democrático Revolucionario, the 'respectable' political front of the communist-controlled guerrillas in El Salvador. The choice of initials, FDR, with their echoes of President Franklin Delano Roosevelt, is believed not to be fortuitous.*
FMLN: Frente Farabundo Martí de Liberación Nacional of El Salvador. Named after a Cuban nationalist leader, who died in 1895, the FMLN is the main umbrella organisation of the guerrillas.

This document is marred by certain typing errors requiring clarification. Thus (Chancellor Bruno) Kreisky of Austria's name is spelt 'Kryski' and 'Braudl' of Germany can only be Brandt. Again 'Horgo' of Italia is presumably Pietro Longo, leader of the Partito Socialista Democrático. It was submitted by Chris de Rigg, who represented the NJM at the meeting.

REPORT ON MEETING OF SECRET REGIONAL CAUCUS OF
[word missing] HELD IN MANAGUA FROM
6TH—7TH JANUARY, 1983

The following Organizations were represented:-

F.S.L.N.	— Nicaragua	—	Antonio Marguin [Jarquin]
M.N.R.	— El Salvador	—	Hector Oqueli
R.P.	— Chile	—	Freda
P.N.P.	— Jamaica	—	Paul Miller
P.C.C.	— Cuba	—	Silva
N.J.M.	— Grenada	—	Chris DeRiggs

. . . .

I. ANALYSIS

i) Regional Situation—the progressive forces are in control.

a) There are fourteen members of the S.I. Committee for Latin America and the Caribbean.

Of these fourteen, there are seven parties that are generally progressive and some within a Marxist-Lennist trend.

There are three (3) new parties that have recently gained consultative observer status in S.I. They are:

(i). Puerto Rico.

(ii). W.P.A.-Guyana

(iii)P.L.P.-St. Lucia

The presence of these parties will help to strengthen the influence of the progressive forces within the Regional Committee. These parties can, in effect, function like full members of the organization. We must always consult with them and keep them informed.

2. EUROPE IN RELATION TO LATIN AMERICA

a) There are sharp divisions among the European parties in their outlook on Latin America.

b) Our friends in this area are prepared to accept the Latin American Revolutionary process as being palatable if restricted to the Latin American context.

c) There is a great amount of misunderstanding about Latin America both among our friends and our enemies—some amount of fear and uncertainty.

d) Many of the European S.I. parties expect us to understand the concept of "the Soviet Menace".

e) Some European parties are concerned that, by the Latin American presence in S.I., they have let in a [illeg.]

f) Many European Parties are willing to hold discussions with us at levels which indicate the contradictions among themselves -

—the difference between Kryski of Austria and Braudl of Germany on the P.L.O. question.

g) Our strongest allies in Europe are the Nordic S.I. parties and that of Holland. There is also good potential with the U.D.P. of Canada.

h) Our principal enemies are to be found among the parties of Soares and Horgo in Portugal and Italy respectively—the Social Democrats of the U.S.A. are also our sworn enemies.

i) The reason why the European parties did not allow W.P.A. and P.L.P. to get beyond the consultative membership status is because of their fear of the growth of membership with parties that they do not control.

j) A Mission to Europe comprising of our most trusted forces in Latin America and the Caribbean can be strategically valuable before the Sydney Congress. It can help to assure our friends and confuse our enemies.

DECISIONS

1. The next meeting of the Broad Latin America Region S.I. Committee will be in any one of the following places:-

Las Paz - Bolivia
Mexico
Caracas
Canada

Michael Manley of P.N.P. and Anselmo Sule of P.R. will co-ordinate with B. Carlson of the S.I. Secretariat on this matter. Member parties will be informed accordingly.

2. A Broad resolution on the Latin American and Caribbean situation will be passed at the meeting of the Regional Committee.

   Agenda for this meeting will include:

   a) Analysis of current political situation.

   b) Attitudes to S.I. in Latin America

   c) Issues for Sydney:

      i) New situation

      ii) Expansion of S.I.

   d) S.I. Latin America Comtee:

      i)   Structure
      ii) Staff
      iii) Officers

   e) Christian Democracy in Latin America.

   f) Sydney Resolutions.

3. Hector Oquel of M.N.R. of El Salvador will draft a Resolution on Latin America and the Caribbean by 31st January, 1983. This Resolution will be specifically for the Sydney Congress and will address only the most major issues.

   The following guidelines will be the basis for the Resolution:-

   (a) The Basle Resolution - including such themes like Peace and Non-Intervention, Anti-Militarisation in the Region, Anti-dictatorship, the settlement of disputes, etc.

   (b) Solidarity with Nicaragua, Grenada and the F.D.R., F.M.L.N. and M.N.R. of El Salvador.

(c) A limited number of other key issues in the Region.

(d) The creation of a platform and frame of reference in S.I., the approach on the Latin America and Caribbean Region until the next Congress in Belgium (in the subsequent 2 years).

4. Subject to the approval of N.J.M., the next meeting of the Secret Regional Caucus of progressive S.I. parties will be in Grenada around the 13th and 14th March. This meeting will have strategic value in that it will provide the opportunity to:

   i) Assess the results of the tour of Europe by the selected parties, and

   ii) Conduct a final assessment on issues related to the Sydney Congress—questions of tactics and levels of co-ordination can also be discussed.

(No paragraph 5 in the original.)

6. Grenada should consider inviting a few key S.I. personalities to March 13th celebrations.

7. Bilaterals will be held with new Regional S.I. forces before Congress—Grenada will speak with W.P.A. and P.L.P.

8. In the meeting in Grenada, we are going to consider what initiatives can be taken to support Surinam. If the Surinam Government wishes, an unofficial familiarization visit can be organized subsequent to proposed Grenada meeting. This it is felt, may have value in preparing members of the Regional Caucus to be able to speak with authority if the question of Surinam is raised in Sydney. If a decision is made to go ahead with this, the team can comprise:
   Radical Party of Chile
   F.S.L.N.
   P.N.P.
   N.D.P.

   N.J.M. will establish contact with Surinam and guide the Regional Secret Caucus accordingly.

At the meeting of the S.I. Resolution Committee and Finance Committee in Madrid and Italy respectively during the middle of February, Regional parties should try to have the possible presence.

Subsequent to the Madrid and Italy meetings, a tour of Europe should be organized to hold Bilaterals with all European parties who belong to S.I.

The participants of this mission should include:
Ungo of M.N.R.
Oquel of M.N.R.
Sule of P.R.
Manley of P.N.P.
Miller of P.N.P.
A senior representative of N.J.M.

This mission will seek to counter the forces of Portugal, Italy and the U.S.A.

Seek to spreak discussion within hostile European parties.

Work of the expulsion of the (C.I.A.) U.S.A. Social Democratic Party.

9. Progressive S.I. forces in the Region should seek to attend COPKAL meeting scheduled for Brazil in March and secure reinforcement of Sydney S.I.L.A. Resolution.

10. To push ahead and implement the proposal for the establishment of a Regional Institute for Political and Economic Research.

—Paul Miller of Jamaica as Director
—Open bank account in the Bahamas with signatures of Miller and Hector Oquel.

Maintain the Secret Regional Caucus with periodic and special meetings.

Review membership in the future.

Submitted by
CDE. CHRIS DE RIGGS.